teens cook

DESSERT

Teens Cook

Cook

DESSERT

Megan and Jill Carle

WITH JUDI CARLE

TEN SPEED PRESS
Berkeley | Toronto

Ten Speed Press
Box 7123
Berkeley, California 94707
www.tenspeed.com

Distributed in Australia by Simon and Schuster Australia, in Canada by Ten Speed Press
Canada, in New Zealand by Southern Publishers Group, in South Africa by Real Books,
and in the United Kingdom and Europe by Airlift Book Company.

Cover and text design by Toni Tajima
Food styling by Liesl Maggiore

Library of Congress Cataloging-in-Publication Data

Carle, Megan.
  Teens cook dessert / Megan and Jill Carle, with Judi Carle.
    p. cm.
  ISBN-13: 978-1-58008-752-0
  ISBN-10: 1-58008-752-3
  1. Desserts. I. Carle, Jill. II. Carle, Judi. III. Title.
  TX773.C342 2006
  641.8'6--dc22

                         2005024343

Printed in China
First printing, 2006

1 2 3 4 5 6 7 8 9 10 - 10 09 08 07 06

DeDicaTiON

While we're sure there are dozens of people we could
dedicate a book of desserts to, we decided the most fitting
was our grandfather Bob. From his insatiable sweet tooth
to his nearly world-famous popcorn, he was a true food
lover who would never even consider skipping the most
important meal of the day, dessert. He was our inspiration
for attempting to create unusual desserts, and no matter
how weird it was, his eyes would twinkle with pleasure
and he would eat every bite.

After our first book came out, we questioned the need
for publicity, as our grandfather was taking care of it, one
person at a time. We figure he did a good job because we
asked to write one book and they let us write two. What
a bargain! And he would have loved that too.

We love you and miss you.

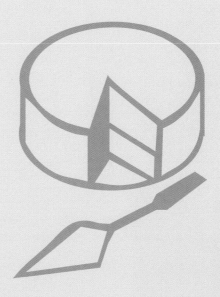

Contents

Acknowledgments

To Lorena Jones, publisher extraordinaire, Toni Tajima, designer par excellence, and the most outstanding editor, Lily Binns (whose name should be a *Harry Potter* character) go our undying gratitude. You believed in our books, asked for our opinions and actually listened, and treated us with respect. Be careful, we could get used to that.

Many thanks to Jessica Boone and Liesl Maggiore. You made our food look great, put up with the heat and the endless musicals blaring on the television, and still managed to make the photo shoot fun.

You are the best.

M

Yvonne Govea, we salute you! Anyone who can put up with our nonsense, clean up our messes, and keep our mom sane through this whole process deserves a medal. And to Jim Govea, thanks for taking one for the team. We know it was tough eating all those desserts, but someone had to do it.

To our friends Patrick, Elvin, Robin, Amber, Tommy, Noelle, Nick, and Emily, we knew you were good friends, but sitting out-side for photos in 116-degree heat goes above and beyond. We promise if we do this again it will be in January.

And always last, but never least, thanks Dad! You are our number one taste tester, put up with our messes, deal with our moods, and still manage to offer encouragement. What more could we ask for . . . well, maybe a car?

Introduction

We love making desserts. That's how we got interested in cooking and it's still what we like best. We started helping our mom in the kitchen when we were three. (Although calling it helping is probably a huge exaggeration.) Of course, we only wanted to help with the fun stuff like cookies and cakes. When we finally learned to follow a recipe by ourselves, the fun really started. No recipe was safe.

We went through the food-coloring stage, when nothing could be its natural color. We made blue cakes, red cookies, green cupcakes, cakes with different colored layers, and even cakes with two colors swirled together. Then we moved on to candy. We chopped up every type of candy imaginable to add to cookies. Some of them, like the Malted Milk Ball Cookies, became family favorites. Others were not so successful. (Did you know gummy bears melt in the oven? They looked so sad.)

Around that time, our mom began editing cookbooks and the world of fine-dining desserts and pastries was opened up to us. We were the only ten- and twelve-year-olds on the block who came home from school and made tuiles. In fact, we were probably the only kids on the block who even knew what tuiles were. As with most kids that age, we were fearless. We made them in all different flavors and rolled, folded, and twisted them into any shape we could think of. We learned to make ice cream and sorbet. We learned about ganache and anglaise. We learned to use phyllo dough, puff pastry, and other kinds of dough. And then came the most revolutionary idea we had heard yet, individual desserts. We really latched on to that one. We layered things, stuffed things, and put together some of the most interesting combinations you can imagine. By the time we were thirteen and fifteen, we were making so many desserts that our mom called a local homeless shelter and they began picking them up every week.

The good news is that even though our passion for baking hasn't cooled, we have learned a lot about which combinations work and, more importantly, which ones don't. We've toned down our experimenting and come to realize that a lot of the classic food combinations are really good. (Which would be why they became classic in the first place.) Our experimenting shifted from trying to reinvent the wheel to making adjustments to old favorites and taking pieces of different recipes and putting them together in different ways.

We have compiled a variety of old family recipes, some things we concocted over the years, and a few recipes that we came up with just for this book. We tried to come up with a good mix of traditional stuff, cool stuff, and fun stuff. (Those are technical terms.) Many of the recipes are very simple and a few not so simple. But don't let the more involved recipes scare you. As our dad always says, "No guts, no glory." Read through the whole recipe first, then just take it one step at a time. It may not be perfect the first time, but you'll get there. And if not, maybe you'll make food history. When you read the kitchen history sidebars, you'll be surprised to find out how many common desserts are the results of mistakes or accidents.

Although we love to make great desserts, we are basically lazy. That means if we're making a pie and there is a store-bought piecrust in the refrigerator, we'll use it. But if we don't have one, we'll make it from scratch because it's easier than driving to the store to get one. The kitchen shortcut sidebars reflect this attitude, and they are things we may do depending on the day, the time, our mood, or the weather. In other words, sometimes we use them, sometimes we don't. Feel free to do the same. Unlike math class, we don't require you to show your work; the end result is all that matters.

So go ahead—pick a recipe and give it a try!

Megan and Jill

ThiNGS YOU SHOULD KNOW ABOUT iNGReDieNTS

We didn't say this in the recipes because it would have gotten really boring and wasted a lot of space, but wash all **vegetables** and **fruit** before using them. We don't even want to think about what they have been sprayed with and how many grubby hands have touched them.

Freshly squeezed lemon juice has a fresher flavor than the bottled version. That said, if we have fresh lemons in the house, we use them. If not, we use the bottled stuff. And truthfully, sometimes when we have fresh lemons we still use the bottled stuff because it's easier. Use whichever one you feel like using.

We say **butter** or **spray the pan** in the recipes. We always spray. It's faster, it's fat free, and you don't have to get your hands all greasy.

All the **eggs** in the recipes are large. Everything else is medium unless we state differently. In other words, if we say "large apple," we mean a large apple. If we just say "apple," we mean medium. That goes for cookware, too; when we say just "a bowl," we mean a medium-size bowl.

For other kinds of recipes we use low-fat **sour cream** and **cream cheese**, but for baking you must use the regular kind. Using the low-fat versions in baking messes up the recipes and you will end up with fallen cakes and cheesecakes that are so crevassed they resemble the moon.

We only use **brand-name pure vanilla extract**. The imitation stuff just doesn't have the same flavor, and Joe's pure vanilla that you buy for $3.00 a pint at the flea market will make your food an unappetizing muddy-gray color. Not, of course, that we would have tried to cheap out like that. Okay, maybe we did once.

We use **salted butter** for a very good reason. That's what our mom buys. Since we are both poor college students this year, we learned that butter is really expensive. We also learned that the cheapest place to get it is out of Mom's freezer. So salted butter it is.

We almost always use **Granny Smith apples**. They are okay for eating, great for baking, and available year-round. That doesn't mean that they are the only apples you can use. **McIntosh**, **Golden Delicious**, and **Jonathans** are also great for baking.

We refuse to get into the **shortening-versus-butter-in-piecrust** argument. We have tried it both ways and even half and half, and we honestly can't tell the difference. Use whichever you want.

When we say **chocolate chips,** we mean **semisweet**. If we mean any other kind, we will specifically mention it.

This note will make many pastry chefs cry, but here goes nothing. For **semisweet chocolate**, we use **chocolate chips**; for **unsweetened**, **German**, and **white chocolate**, we use the kind that comes in a **box full of 1-ounce squares**. We go through at least 10 pounds of chocolate a month, and the really good stuff is too expensive for us to use on a regular basis. Occasionally, we will use it for something special, and it is great, but the reality is that our friends don't have discerning enough palates to tell the difference.

This one doesn't have anything to do with ingredients, but it is something you need to know. **Make sure you scrape the bowl when you are mixing ingredients**. We didn't put this in the recipes because it seemed a little silly to have about two hundred scrape-the-bowl instructions. So when the ingredients are all over the sides of the bowl, scrape them back in with a rubber spatula.

Cookies, Bars, and Stuff

I love chocolate chip cookies and think that no dessert cookbook would be complete without at least one recipe for them. This version takes a little more time than the recipe listed on bags of chocolate chips, but these cookies are worth every second. The oatmeal makes them thick and soft so they taste like the ones you get at the stores in the mall.

CHOCOLATE CHIP COOKIES

MAKES ABOUT 5 DOZEN COOKIES

2½ cups rolled oats

4 ounces milk chocolate

1 cup butter

1 cup sugar

1 cup firmly packed brown sugar

2 eggs

1 teaspoon vanilla

1 teaspoon baking powder

1 teaspoon baking soda

2 cups flour

2 cups chocolate chips

Preheat the oven to 375°F.

Place the oatmeal in a blender or food processor and pulse until finely powdered.

Chop the milk chocolate into small pieces.

Place the butter, sugar, and brown sugar in a large bowl and mix with an electric mixer on low speed for 2 minutes, or until creamy. Add the eggs and vanilla and mix for 1 minute, or until completely combined. Add the baking powder and baking soda and mix for 30 seconds. Add the flour and oatmeal and mix for 2 minutes, or until completely incorporated. Add the chopped chocolate and chocolate chips and mix for 30 seconds, or until the chips are fairly well distributed.

Spoon golf ball–sized balls of the dough about 3 inches apart on ungreased baking sheets and bake for 12 minutes, or until just set in the middle. Remove the cookies from the pan and cool on parchment or waxed paper.

KITCHEN HISTORY

This may possibly be the world's greatest mistake. Ruth and Kenneth Wakefield ran the Toll House Inn near Whitman, Massachusetts. In 1937, Ruth broke up a chocolate bar and mixed it into her cookie batter thinking everything would mix together and make chocolate cookies. Needless to say, it didn't work out that way, but chocolate chip cookies were born.

MALTED MILK BALL COOKIES

These are my sister Mindy's favorite cookies. She knows that if she really wants them, she needs to show up with a bag of malted milk balls. Otherwise, the only time she can be guaranteed to get them is right after Easter, when we have lots of malted milk ball eggs. They have a little less chocolate around them, but they make the cookies really colorful.

MAKES ABOUT 4 DOZEN COOKIES

2 cups malted milk balls

1 cup butter

³/₄ cup sugar

³/₄ cup firmly packed brown sugar

2 eggs

1 teaspoon vanilla

¹/₄ cup malted milk powder

1 teaspoon baking soda

2 cups flour

Place the malted milk balls in a resealable bag and gently hit them several times with a rolling pin or the bottom of a pan. (They should be broken into chunks with a little bit of crumbs, not completely pulverized.)

Place the butter, sugar, and brown sugar in a large bowl and mix with an electric mixer on medium speed for 2 minutes, or until completely combined. Add the eggs and vanilla and mix on medium-high speed for 2 minutes, or until fluffy. Add the malted milk powder and baking soda and mix on low speed for 1 minute, or until just combined. Add the flour and mix on low speed for 1 minute. Add the smashed malted milk balls and mix for 1 minute, or until just combined. Refrigerate the dough for at least 1 hour.

Preheat the oven to 350°F.

Drop tablespoonfuls of the dough onto ungreased baking sheets at least 3 inches apart (they spread a lot). Bake for 8 to 10 minutes, or until they just begin to brown on the edges. Remove the cookies from the pan immediately and cool on parchment or waxed paper.

✳ Kitchen Tip ✳

Have you ever opened your brown sugar and found a big hard lump? Well, all is not lost. If you put a piece of bread in with the brown sugar and seal it tightly, the sugar will soften again.

These are better than your average peanut butter cookies because they have a surprise in the middle. I came up with this idea after seeing a recipe for peanut butter and jelly ice cream sandwiches, and they quickly became a family favorite. You can use any flavor of jam; just make sure to seal the bottom of the cookies really well so they don't leak.

M

PEANUT BUTTER AND JELLY COOKIES

MAKES ABOUT 2 DOZEN COOKIES

½ cup butter

¾ cup peanut butter

1¼ cups firmly packed
brown sugar

1 egg

3 tablespoons milk

¾ teaspoon baking soda

2 cups flour

¼ cup jelly or jam

Preheat the oven to 350°F.

Place the butter, peanut butter, and brown sugar in a large bowl and mix with an electric mixer on medium speed for 2 minutes, or until completely combined. Add the egg and milk and mix on medium speed for 2 minutes, or until light and fluffy. Add the baking soda and mix for 30 seconds. Add the flour and mix until completely incorporated.

Roll the dough into golf ball–sized balls. Holding a ball in the palm of your hand, press your thumb in the center to form a deep hole. Spoon about ½ teaspoon of the jam into the hole and pinch the top closed. Gently

roll the dough back into a ball shape and place seam side down on an ungreased baking sheet. Repeat with the remaining balls and place 3 inches apart on the baking sheet. Bake for 15 to 18 minutes, or until lightly browned on the edges. Remove the cookies from the pan immediately and cool on parchment or waxed paper.

KITCHEN HISTORY

Peanut butter was known as early as 1200 A.D., when the ancient Incas were known to make peanuts into a paste. The creamy version that we are used to came to be in 1928, when Joseph Rosenfield invented a churning process that made it smooth. Interestingly enough, he licensed his idea to the makers of Peter Pan peanut butter, but four years later started his own brand, which he called Skippy. That hardly seems fair.

These simple sugar cookies are the first cookies anyone in our family learns to make. I started making them with my niece, Emmy, when she was four. She liked to press the cookies down with the glass. Now that she just turned six, she only needs help with the measurements and the baking.

MILLION-DOLLAR COOKIES

MAKES ABOUT 6 DOZEN COOKIES

1 cup butter

½ cup sugar plus extra for dipping

½ cup firmly packed brown sugar

1 egg

1 teaspoon vanilla

¼ teaspoon baking soda

2 cups flour

Preheat the oven to 350°F.

Place the butter, sugar, and brown sugar in a large bowl and mix with an electric mixer on low speed for 1 minute, or until creamy. Add the egg and vanilla and mix on medium speed for 2 minutes, or until fluffy. Add the baking soda and flour and mix on low speed for 1 minute, or until completely combined.

Drop teaspoonfuls of the dough onto ungreased baking sheets at least 2 inches apart. Pour a little sugar in a small bowl. Press the bottom of a glass in the dough to get it sticky and then dip it into the sugar. Press the cookies about ¼ inch thick with the sugared glass, dipping the glass in the sugar after each cookie. Bake for 10 to 12 minutes, or until lightly golden brown. Remove the cookies from the pan and cool on parchment or waxed paper.

✳ Kitchen Tip ✳

If you don't have any brown sugar in the house, you can substitute granulated sugar and molasses. For each cup of brown sugar you need, use 1 cup of granulated sugar plus 1 tablespoon molasses.

These may be the best brownies ever. I know they take more time than just opening a package of mix, but they are so much better than anything you will ever get out of a box. Besides, if you make them from scratch, you have legitimate bragging rights. And no, adding eggs and oil does not constitute making something from scratch.

TURTLE BROWNIES

MAKES 24 BROWNIES

BROWNIES

4 ounces unsweetened chocolate

1 cup butter

2 cups sugar

4 eggs

2 teaspoons vanilla

1 teaspoon baking powder

1 cup flour

CARAMEL

1¼ cups heavy cream

1¼ cups sugar

6 tablespoons corn syrup

⅛ teaspoon cream of tartar

¼ cup butter

½ teaspoon vanilla

1 cup pecans

Preheat the oven to 350°F. Lightly butter or spray a 9 by 13-inch baking pan.

To prepare the brownies: Place the chocolate and butter in a large microwave-safe bowl and microwave on high heat for 1 minute. Stir the mixture until the chocolate is melted and the butter is completely incorporated. If the chocolate is not all melted, place it back in the microwave for 15 seconds at a time, stirring after each time, until it is completely melted. Be careful not to let the chocolate start to bubble or it will burn and get gritty. Stir in the sugar. Add the eggs one at a time, stirring well after each addition. Stir in the vanilla and baking powder. Add the flour and stir until just combined.

Spread two thirds of the batter into the prepared pan and set aside.

Meanwhile, prepare the caramel: Place the cream, sugar, corn syrup, and cream of tartar in a saucepan and cook over medium-high heat, stirring occasionally, for 15 minutes, or until it reaches 246°F. (Don't panic if the caramel seems too light. It should be a very pale yellow color, not even close to the color of the kind you buy in the store.)

KITCHEN SHORTCUT

Use 2 cups of prepared caramel sauce and omit the caramel ingredients and preparation.

Remove the pan from the heat, stir in the butter and vanilla, and set aside.

Place the brownie pan in the oven and bake for 20 minutes.

Coarsely chop the pecans.

Pour the caramel over the partially cooked brownies. Sprinkle the pecans over the caramel and drop the remaining brownie batter by teaspoonfuls around the pan, but do not spread it out. (The remaining batter will not cover all of the caramel.) Cook for 18 minutes, or until the batter on top is set. Cool completely and cut into 2-inch squares.

✳ Kitchen Tip ✳

If you don't have a candy thermometer, or if you are like us and just don't trust it, there is another way to check if your candy is ready. Dip a clean spoon in the boiling syrup and drop a small amount of the syrup into a glass of ice-cold water. You can then test with your fingers to see if it has reached the right consistency.

Soft-ball stage	236°F	Forms a ball that flattens when removed from the water.
Firm-ball stage	244°F	Forms a firm ball that doesn't flatten when removed from the water.
Hard-ball stage	254°F	Forms a ball that is hard enough to hold its shape, yet is still elastic.
Soft-crack stage	270°F	Separates into threads that are hard, but not brittle.
Hard-crack stage	300°F	Separates into threads that are hard and brittle.

✳✳ Kitchen Tip

If you don't have unsweetened chocolate in the house, you can substitute 3 tablespoons of cocoa and 1 tablespoon of vegetable oil for each ounce of chocolate.

We were forever trying out different coconut macaroon recipes because they are my Grandma Carle's favorite cookie. After making just about every recipe we could find, we tweaked a couple things and came up with this: a melt-in-your-mouth cookie with a light coconut flavor.

M

COCONUT MACAROONS

MAKES ABOUT 2 DOZEN COOKIES

2 egg whites

Pinch of salt

³/₄ cup sugar

1 teaspoon vanilla

1¹/₂ cups sweetened coconut

Preheat the oven to 350°F. Lightly butter or spray a baking sheet.

Place the egg whites and salt in a large bowl and beat with an electric mixer on high speed for 1 minute, or until frothy. Gradually add the sugar, beating at high speed for 3 minutes, or until stiff peaks form. (When the beaters are lifted out of the egg whites, they form peaks that remain upright.) Fold in the vanilla and coconut. Drop teaspoonfuls of the batter onto the prepared baking sheet at least 2 inches apart and bake for 12 to 15 minutes, or until lightly browned. Cool for 1 minute and remove from the pan. Cool completely on parchment or waxed paper and store in an airtight container.

KITCHEN HISTORY

Although the first cookie-like cakes are thought to date back to seventh-century Persia, the cookies that we know and love were brought to America by the Dutch. Dutch bakers used small amounts of cake batter to test the oven temperature before baking a large cake. These test cakes were called *koekje*, meaning "little cake" in Dutch.

LeMoN BARS

These are one of our family favorites—a requirement on any tray of cookies or bars. They hold up really well, so they can be made a day or two before you serve them.

MAKES 24 BARS

CRUST

2 cups flour

¹⁄₂ cup confectioners' sugar

1 cup butter

FILLING

4 eggs

2 cups sugar

¹⁄₄ cup flour

1 teaspoon baking powder

¹⁄₄ cup lemon juice

GLAZE

1 cup confectioners' sugar

3 tablespoons lemon juice

To prepare the crust: Preheat the oven to 350°F.

Place the flour, confectioners' sugar, and butter in a large bowl and mix with an electric mixer on low speed for 2 minutes, or until crumbly. Press the mixture into the bottom of an ungreased 9 by 13-inch pan and bake for 20 to 30 minutes, or until lightly brown. Leave the oven on at 350°F.

To prepare the filling: Place the eggs, sugar, flour, and baking powder in a medium bowl and stir until combined. Add the lemon juice and stir until completely smooth. Pour the mixture over the warm crust and bake for 25 to 30 minutes, or until the top is golden brown. Let cool completely.

To prepare the glaze: Place the confectioners' sugar and lemon juice in a small bowl and stir until smooth.

Smooth the glaze over the bars, let set for 30 minutes, and then cut into 2-inch squares.

✳ Kitchen Tip ✳

As picky as it may seem, there is a difference between liquid and dry measuring cups. Dry measuring cups usually come in a stack with varying sizes. Liquid measuring cups come in 1-, 2-, and 4-cup sizes and have pour spouts. They are not interchangeable. Measuring 1 cup of liquid in a dry measuring cup can make a difference of almost an ounce. It may not seem like much, but it can easily throw off a cake recipe.

This is a recipe that has been in our family for several generations. Whenever we have a get-together with my mom's family, one of my great-aunts is guaranteed to bring these bars. I have no problem with that; I mean, what could be better than apple pie you can eat with your hands?

APPLE SLICES

MAKES 24 BARS

CRUST

2 cups flour

3 tablespoons sugar

3/4 cup cold butter or shortening

3 tablespoons milk

1 egg yolk

FILLING

4 cups peeled and thinly sliced apples (about 6)

3/4 cup sugar

1/2 teaspoon ground cinnamon

1 tablespoon cornstarch

2 tablespoons lemon juice

1 egg white

GLAZE

1 cup confectioners' sugar

2 tablespoons milk

To prepare the crust: Preheat the oven to 350°F.

Stir together the flour and sugar in a large bowl. Add the butter and cut in with a pastry cutter or two knives until the mixture is the size of small peas. Add the milk and egg yolk and blend gently with a fork until the dough just starts to hold together. (If you prefer to use a food processor, place the flour, sugar, and butter in the bowl of a food processor and pulse for about 10 seconds, or until crumbly. Add the milk and egg yolk and pulse until the dough just forms a ball.) Form the dough into two 1/2-inch-thick disks and place one on a lightly floured work surface. Roll out the dough into an 11 by 15-inch rectangle and place it in the bottom and about 1 inch up the sides of an ungreased 9 by 13-inch pan. Roll out the remaining dough into a 9 by 13-inch rectangle and set aside.

To prepare the filling: Place the apples, sugar, cinnamon, cornstarch, and lemon juice in a large bowl and stir until well combined.

Spread the apple mixture evenly over the crust. Place the remaining crust over the apples and press all around the edges to seal the two pieces of dough together. Trim any excess dough from the edges of the pan. Lightly beat the egg white with a fork and brush over the dough. Bake for 45 minutes, or until the apples are tender and the crust is golden brown. Remove from the oven and cool completely.

To prepare the glaze: Combine the confectioners' sugar and milk in a small bowl.

Spread the glaze over the top crust, then cut into 2-inch squares.

KiTCHEN MATH

Here is a small but important piece of kitchen math that we use all the time when doubling or cutting recipes in half.

3 teaspoons = 1 tablespoon
16 tablespoons = 1 cup

So when you are cutting a recipe in half and it originally calls for ³/₄ cup, you will know that you will need only 6 tablespoons because if 1 cup = 16 tablespoons, then ³/₄ cup = 12 table-spoons, and half of 12 is 6.

These bars are a really easy alternative to cheesecake. The shortbread crust is sturdy enough to make them easy to handle but still melts in your mouth. I usually use raspberry or blueberry jam, but you can use whatever flavor you like.

M

CHEESECAKE BARS

MAKES 16 BARS:

CRUST

¹/₃ cup butter

¹/₃ cup firmly packed brown sugar

1 cup flour

FILLING

8 ounces cream cheese

¹/₄ cup sugar

2 tablespoons milk

1 tablespoon lemon juice

¹/₂ teaspoon vanilla

1 egg

¹/₂ cup jam, any flavor

To prepare the crust: Preheat the oven to 350°F.

Place the butter and brown sugar in a bowl and mix with an electric mixer on low speed for 1 minute, or until fluffy. Add the flour and mix for 1 minute, or until just combined. Press the dough into the bottom of an ungreased 8-inch square pan and bake for 10 minutes, or until lightly browned.

To prepare the filling: Place the cream cheese and sugar in a large bowl and mix with an electric mixer on low speed for 2 minutes, or until smooth. Add the milk, lemon juice, vanilla, and egg and mix for 1 minute, or until thoroughly combined.

Spread the mixture over the baked crust and drop tablespoonfuls of the jam on the filling. Run a knife back and forth through the filling to distribute the jam, being careful not to cut into the crust. Bake for 25 minutes, or until lightly browned. Cool completely and cut into 2-inch squares.

WHITE CHOCOLATE-MACADAMIA NUT BLONDIES

I think these are a perfect alternative to brownies. They have the texture of brownies without all of the chocolate. Here I use white chocolate and macadamia nuts, but they are also great with butterscotch, chocolate, or peanut butter chips and any kind of nuts.

MAKES 24 BLONDIES

Preheat the oven to 350°F. Lightly butter or spray a 9 by 13-inch baking pan.

Combine the butter and brown sugar in a large bowl and stir until combined. Add the eggs and vanilla and stir until completely blended. Add the flour and baking powder and stir until there are no visible streaks of flour. Stir in the white chocolate chips and nuts. Pour the batter into the prepared baking pan and spread evenly. Bake for 20 minutes, or until a toothpick inserted in the center comes out clean. Cool completely and cut into 2-inch squares.

³/₄ cup butter, melted

1¹/₂ cups firmly packed brown sugar

2 eggs

³/₄ teaspoon vanilla

2¹/₄ cups flour

1¹/₂ teaspoons baking powder

¹/₂ cup white chocolate chips

¹/₂ cup macadamia nuts

✳ Kitchen Tip ✳

Out of baking powder or baking soda? You can use baking powder in place of baking soda (you'll need 4 times as much and it may affect the taste), but you can't use baking soda in place of powder. Baking soda by itself lacks the acidity to make a cake rise. However, you can use ¹/₂ teaspoon of cream of tartar and ¹/₄ teaspoon of baking soda for each teaspoon of baking powder.

I was not a biscotti fan and didn't want to include it in this book. When my sister was making it, I tried the dough and it was gross. I tried it after it baked the first time and it was way too chocolaty. When it was finished I tried it again, and I'm not sure what happened, but it was really good. I guess I am now a biscotti fan.

TRIPLE-CHOCOLATE BISCOTTI

MAKES ABOUT 40 PIECES

1½ cups almonds

2 cups flour

1¼ cups cocoa

1½ teaspoons baking soda

¼ teaspoon salt

2 cups sugar

¾ cup chocolate chips

5 eggs

1½ teaspoons vanilla

6 ounces white chocolate

Preheat the oven to 325°F.

Place the almonds on a baking sheet and toast in the oven for 10 to 15 minutes, or until lightly browned.

Lightly butter or spray 2 baking sheets.

Place the almonds, flour, cocoa, baking soda, salt, sugar, and chocolate chips in a large bowl and stir until combined. Place the eggs and vanilla in a small bowl and beat until combined. Using an electric mixer on low speed, gradually mix the eggs into the flour until the dough comes together. Place the dough on a lightly floured surface and divide it into 4 pieces. Lightly flour your hands and roll each piece into a log about 10 inches long and 2 inches in diameter. Place 2 of the logs on each baking sheet and bake for 30 to 35 minutes, or until the sides are firm and the tops are cracked. Remove the baking sheets from the oven and let cool for 15 minutes. Lower the oven temperature to 300°F.

Cut the logs slightly on the diagonal into ½- to ¾-inch-thick slices. Place the slices flat on the baking

KITCHEN HISTORY

Although the earliest records date biscuits back to second-century Rome, early seamen's biscuits, known as hardtack, were probably the first modern version of biscotti. Their dryness made them resistant to mold for as long as four months. We do know they were a favorite of Christopher Columbus, who relied on them as a staple food for his fifteenth-century sea voyages.

sheets and bake for 25 minutes. Remove from the oven and cool completely.

Place the white chocolate in a microwave-safe bowl and microwave on high heat for 1 minute, then stir. If the chocolate is not all melted, place it back in the microwave for 15 seconds at a time, stirring after each time, until it is completely melted. Using a spoon, drizzle the white chocolate over the biscotti and let stand until the chocolate hardens. Store in an airtight container for up to 1 month.

Cakes, Pies, and Stuff

This is the best carrot cake I have ever tasted. Although it looks complicated, the ingredients just get put in a bowl and stirred. Okay, so grating the carrots is kind of a pain, but after you try this cake, you'll believe me when I say it is totally worth the time.

CARROT CAKE WITH CREAM CHEESE FROSTING

SERVES 12

CAKE

$^3/_4$ cup walnuts

4 eggs

$1^1/_3$ cups vegetable oil

$1^3/_4$ cups grated carrots (4 or 5)

1 cup crushed pineapple, drained

$^1/_2$ cup sweetened coconut

$^1/_4$ cup raisins

1 teaspoon baking soda

1 tablespoon baking powder

$^1/_2$ teaspoon salt

$1^1/_2$ tablespoons ground cinnamon

$1^3/_4$ cups sugar

$2^1/_3$ cups flour

To prepare the cake: Preheat the oven to 350°F. Lightly butter or spray a 9 by 13-inch baking pan.

Roughly chop the walnuts and place them in a large bowl. Add the eggs and beat lightly to break them up. Add the vegetable oil, carrots, pineapple, coconut, and raisins and stir until combined. Add the baking soda, baking powder, salt, cinnamon, and sugar and stir well. Add the flour and stir until completely incorporated. Pour the batter into the prepared pan and bake for 45 to 55 minutes, or until the center springs back when lightly pressed. Remove the cake from the oven and let cool completely.

✳ Kitchen Tip ✳

Have you ever noticed that raisins, nuts, and chocolate chips sometimes sink to the bottom of the cake? Try tossing them in a little bit of flour before adding them to the batter. The flour will absorb some of the oil and water and keep them from slipping to the bottom.

FROSTING

8 ounces cream cheese

2 tablespoons butter

2 1/2 cups confectioners' sugar

2 tablespoons milk

1 teaspoon vanilla

To prepare the frosting: Place the cream cheese and butter in a large bowl and beat with an electric mixer on medium-high speed for 2 to 3 minutes, or until completely smooth. Add the confectioners' sugar, milk, and vanilla and mix until fluffy.

Spread the frosting over the cooled cake and cut into 3-inch squares.

KITCHEN HISTORY

During the Middle Ages, sweeteners were scarce and expensive in Europe, so people put carrots in cakes and puddings for their sweetness. Although carrot cake didn't become popular in America until the 1950s, we did find a reference to George Washington eating carrot tea cake at Fraunces Tavern in New York on November 25, 1783. He was celebrating British Evacuation Day.

This is one of my favorite recipes from when I was living in Germany. My host mom often served this cake with afternoon tea. I always thought of teatime as being strictly a British custom, but it is also very common in Germany. I have no problem with that. Any excuse to eat dessert in the middle of the day is okay by me. This recipe was originally written in grams, which is how they measure all of their ingredients in Europe, but I converted it so you can make it without the hassle of converting the measurements.

MARBLE POUND CAKE

SERVES 10 TO 12

1⅓ cups butter

1⅓ cups sugar

1 teaspoon vanilla

½ teaspoon salt

5 eggs

4 teaspoons baking powder

3 tablespoons milk

2¾ cups flour

3 tablespoons cocoa

1½ tablespoons sugar

2 tablespoons milk

Preheat the oven to 350°F. Lightly butter or spray a 9-inch loaf pan.

Place the butter and sugar in a large bowl and mix with an electric mixer on medium speed for 1 minute, or until creamy. Add the vanilla and salt and mix for 30 seconds. Add the eggs one at a time, mixing well after each addition. Add the baking powder and milk and mix for 15 seconds. Add the flour and mix for 1 minute, or until completely combined. Pour two thirds of the batter into the prepared pan, reserving the remaining batter for the chocolate cake.

Add the cocoa, sugar, and milk to the remaining batter and stir until combined.

Pour the chocolate batter in the pan and swirl with a fork. Bake for 70 to 80 minutes, or until a toothpick inserted in the center comes out clean. Remove from the pan and cool on a wire rack.

PEACH UPSIDE-DOWN CAKE

> I think upside-down cakes are awesome for two reasons. First, I love the sugary fruit on the top, and second, you don't have to make frosting (as good as frosting is, I hate to make it). I like it best with peaches, but it's also great with pears, plums, or the more traditional pineapple.

SERVES 12

To prepare the topping: Preheat the oven to 350°F.

Put the butter in a 9-inch round baking pan and place it on the stove over medium heat until the butter is mostly melted. Carefully remove the pan from the heat and let cool enough to be able to handle the pan. Add the brown sugar and stir until combined. Smooth the sugar mixture to cover the bottom of the pan. Drain the peach slices, reserving 1/3 cup of the juice for the cake. Arrange the peach slices over the sugar and set aside.

To prepare the cake: Place the eggs in a large bowl and beat with an electric mixer on medium speed for 4 to 5 minutes, or until thick and lemon colored. Add the sugar and mix for 1 minute, or until combined. Add the 1/3 cup reserved peach juice and vanilla and mix for 30 seconds, or until blended. Add the baking powder, salt, and flour and mix for 1 minute, or until just combined. Gently pour the batter into the pan, being careful not to move the peaches around. Bake for 40 to 45 minutes, or until a toothpick inserted into the center comes out clean. Cool for 5 minutes, then run a knife around the edge of the pan to loosen the cake. Place a serving platter upside down on top of the cake and, holding both the pan and the plate, turn them over so the cake drops onto the platter. Let cool for 10 minutes, then remove the pan.

TOPPING

1/4 cup butter

1 cup firmly packed brown sugar

1 (15-ounce) can sliced peaches

CAKE

2 eggs

2/3 cup sugar

1 teaspoon vanilla

1/2 teaspoon baking powder

1/4 teaspoon salt

1 cup flour

We make a lot of angel food cake in our house. We really like it, but we make it so often because we always seem to have extra egg whites. Once when we were using a lot of egg yolks trying different ice cream recipes, we had so many egg whites left, we made five cakes and gave them out as party favors at a family dinner. Not exactly standard party favors, but hey, no one complained.

ANGEL FOOD CAKE WITH TOASTED ALMOND GLAZE

SERVES 10 TO 12

CAKE

1½ cups egg whites (about 12)

1½ teaspoons cream of tartar

¼ teaspoon salt

1½ teaspoons vanilla

½ teaspoon almond extract

1½ cups sugar

¾ cup flour

To prepare the cake: Preheat the oven to 375°F.

Place the egg whites, cream of tartar, salt, vanilla, and almond extract in a large bowl and beat with an electric mixer on high speed for 3 to 4 minutes, or until soft peaks form. (When the beaters are lifted out of the egg whites, they form peaks that fold over when the beaters pull away.) Add the sugar a little at a time and beat until stiff peaks form. Gently fold the flour into the egg whites, ¼ cup at a time, until just blended. Pour the batter into an ungreased tube pan. (If you don't have a tube pan, use two 5 by 9-inch loaf pans.) Cut through the batter with a knife to remove any air bubbles. Bake for 40 to 50 minutes, or until golden brown. Remove the pan from the oven and invert onto the neck of a bottle to cool completely. Lower the oven temperature to 325°F. Once the cake is cooled, run a knife around the edge of the pan to loosen it, then remove it from the pan.

TOPPINGS

½ cup sliced almonds

2 tablespoons butter, melted

1 cup confectioners' sugar

2 tablespoons milk

To prepare the toppings: Spread the almonds on a baking sheet and bake for 10 minutes, or until lightly browned.

Place the butter, confectioners' sugar, and milk in a bowl and stir until smooth.

Spoon half of the glaze on the top of the cooled cake. Sprinkle with the almonds and spoon the remaining glaze over the almonds, allowing it to drip down the sides of the cake.

KITCHEN HISTORY

No one is positive, but historians speculate that angel food cake originated with the Pennsylvania Dutch and evolved as a result of numerous egg whites left over from making noodles. They also believe that the name came about because the cake is so white, light, and fluffy, it must be fit for angels.

I got this recipe from my best friend, Patrick. He told me his grandmother used to make this cake and it was really good. I had to trust him for a while on that one, because every time I made it, the cake disappeared before I had a chance to try it. The rest of my family (and a lot of the neighbors) didn't even bother to wait for it to cool. Once I got to try it, I understood. It's good. No, it's really, really good.

KENTUCKY BUTTER CAKE

SERVES 10 to 12

CAKE

1 cup butter

2 cups sugar

4 eggs

2 tablespoons vanilla

1 teaspoon baking powder

1 teaspoon salt

½ teaspoon baking soda

1 cup sour cream

3 cups flour

To prepare the cake: Preheat the oven to 325°F. Lightly butter or spray a tube or Bundt pan.

Place the butter and sugar in a large bowl and mix with an electric mixer on medium speed for 2 minutes, or until creamy. Add the eggs one at a time, mixing well after each addition. Add the vanilla, baking powder, salt, and baking soda and mix for 1 minute. Alternately add the sour cream and flour, one-third at a time, mixing after each addition. Mix for 3 minutes after all of the sour cream and flour are added. Spoon the batter into the prepared pan and bake for 60 to 75 minutes, or until a toothpick inserted into the center of the cake comes out clean. Remove the cake from the oven and poke holes in the cake with a skewer while it is still warm.

KITCHEN CHEMISTRY

A container of baking powder can last a long time, but when it gets old, it doesn't work so well. If you aren't sure whether yours is fresh or not, place 1 teaspoon of baking powder in 1 cup of hot water. If it bubbles a lot, it is fresh; if not, throw it away.

SAUCE

1 cup sugar

¹/₄ cup water

¹/₂ cup butter

1 tablespoon vanilla

Confectioners' sugar for
dusting

Meanwhile, prepare the sauce: Place the sugar, water, and butter in a small saucepan and cook over medium-high heat for 5 minutes, or until the sugar is dissolved. Add the vanilla and stir until combined.

While the cake is still warm, spoon the sauce over the holes and then allow it to cool completely. Run a knife around the edge of the pan and invert the cooled cake onto a serving platter. Sprinkle with confectioners' sugar.

We always ordered this cake at one of our favorite restaurants. Then they took it off the menu. (I hate when they do that.) So we had to come up with a recipe for it ourselves. When we first started making this cake we used malt powder, but we haven't been able to find it for the last few years, so we switched to malted milk powder. Malt powder gives it a stronger malt flavor, but either way this is a super good cake.

CHOCOLATE MALT CAKE

SERVES 10 TO 12

CAKE

1³/₄ cups flour

2 cups sugar

³/₄ cup cocoa

1 cup malted milk powder

1¹/₂ teaspoons baking soda

1¹/₂ teaspoons baking powder

1 teaspoon salt

2 eggs

1 cup milk

¹/₂ cup vegetable oil

1 teaspoon vanilla

1 cup boiling water

FROSTING

5 ounces unsweetened chocolate

1 cup butter

1 egg

3 cups confectioners' sugar

2 tablespoons malted milk powder

1 teaspoon vanilla

1¹/₂ tablespoons milk

Pinch of salt

12 malted milk balls

To prepare the cake: Preheat the oven to 350°F. Cut two parchment paper circles to fit in the bottom of two 9-inch cake pans and lightly butter or spray the parchment paper and the pan sides.

Combine the flour, sugar, cocoa, malted milk powder, baking soda, baking powder, and salt in a large bowl. Place the eggs in another large bowl and beat well. Add the milk, oil, and vanilla to the eggs and stir until combined. Slowly add the boiling water and mix well. Add the wet ingredients to the flour mixture and stir until smooth. Pour half of the batter into each of the prepared pans and bake for 40 minutes, or until the cake springs back when gently pressed in the center. Remove the cakes from the pans, remove the parchment paper, and place on wire racks to cool.

To prepare the frosting: Place the chocolate in a small microwave-safe bowl and microwave on high heat for 1 minute, then stir. If the chocolate is not all melted, place it back in the microwave for 15 seconds at a time, stirring after each time, until it is completely melted. Be careful not to let the chocolate start to bubble or it will burn and get gritty.

Place the butter and egg in a large bowl and beat with an electric mixer on medium speed for 2 minutes, or until fluffy. Add the confectioners' sugar, malted milk powder, and melted chocolate and mix for 1 minute, or

[continued]

KITCHEN CHEMISTRY

When cakes don't rise enough, your automatic reaction might be to add more baking soda or powder, but that is most likely the exact opposite of what you should do. When you add liquid to baking soda or powder, it forms a gas that creates bubbles. If you have too much of either one, they will create so many small bubbles that larger bubbles break or are unable to form. The smaller bubbles will make your cake more dense. What you want is the larger bubbles to give it a lighter texture. Generally, 1 teaspoon of baking powder or ¼ teaspoon of baking soda per cup of flour will do the trick.

until even in color. Add the vanilla, milk, and salt and mix for 2 minutes, or until fluffy.

To assemble the cake: Place 1 of the cooled cakes upside down on a serving platter and cover the top and sides with half of the frosting. Place the remaining cake upside down on top of the frosted cake and spread the remaining frosting on the top and sides, blending the upper and lower portions of the sides as you go. Arrange the malted milk balls around the outside edge of the cake.

MALT SHOP PIE

My mom has been making this pie every summer since we were little and I've always loved it. With ice cream, malted milk balls, and a chocolate cookie crust, how could it be bad? All I want to know is why we never have it in the winter.

SERVES 6

CRUST

1 cup chocolate cookie crumbs

¼ cup butter, melted

FILLING

1 quart vanilla ice cream

2 cups crushed malted milk balls

TOPPING

½ cup heavy cream

3 tablespoons marshmallow fluff

3 tablespoons malted milk powder

2 tablespoons chocolate milk powder or syrup

KITCHEN SHORTCUT
Use a prepared chocolate cookie crust and omit the crust ingredients and preparation.

To prepare the crust: Place the chocolate cookie crumbs in an ungreased 8- or 9-inch pie pan. Add the butter and stir until combined. Press the mixture on the bottom and up the sides of the pan, using the back of a spoon to flatten the crumbs.

To prepare the filling: Allow the ice cream to soften slightly in the container. Place the ice cream in a large bowl and pour the crushed malted milk balls over the top. Using the back of a spoon, quickly press the malted milk balls into the ice cream, getting them as evenly distributed as possible before the ice cream begins to melt. (If the ice cream gets too soft, it will crystallize when it refreezes.)

Transfer the ice cream to the pie pan, smooth the top with the back of the spoon, and freeze immediately.

To prepare the topping: Place the heavy cream, marshmallow fluff, malted milk powder, and chocolate syrup in a bowl and beat with an electric mixer for 3 to 4 minutes, or until soft peaks form. (When the beaters are lifted out of the cream, they form peaks that fold over as the beaters pull away.)

Spread the topping evenly over the pie and freeze for at least 2 hours, or until ready to serve.

> Apples are my favorite dessert food, hands down. If it has apples, I like it. Therefore, this is one of my favorite pies ever. I particularly like Dutch apple pie because it has the crunchy topping and you only have to make one crust. (Yes, I'm that lazy.)

DUTCH APPLE PIE

SERVES 9

CRUST

- 1 cup flour
- ½ teaspoon salt
- ⅓ cup cold butter or shortening
- 3 tablespoons water

To prepare the crust: Preheat the oven to 375°F.

Stir together the flour and salt in a large bowl. Add the butter and cut in with a pastry cutter or two knives until the mixture is the size of small peas. Add the water and blend gently with a fork until the dough just starts to hold together. (If you prefer to use a food processor, place the flour, salt, and butter in the bowl of a food processor and pulse for about 10 seconds, or until crumbly. Drizzle the water into the food processor while pulsing until the dough just forms a ball.) Form the dough into a ½-inch-thick disk and place it on a lightly floured work surface. Roll the dough into a circle 2 inches

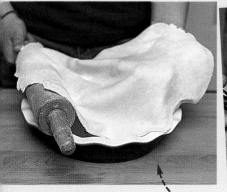

FILLING

6 cups peeled and sliced
   apples (about 8)

1 cup sugar

2 tablespoons flour

½ teaspoon ground cinnamon

1 tablespoon lemon juice

2 tablespoons butter

TOPPING

1½ cups flour

1 cup firmly packed brown
   sugar

1½ teaspoons ground
   cinnamon

¾ cup butter

KITCHEN SHORTCUT

Use 1 prepared piecrust
and omit the crust ingredients and preparation.

larger than your pie pan. Fold the dough in half, or use
a rolling pin, as shown above, and transfer it to the pie
pan. Unfold the dough and gently press it into the pan,
patting out any air pockets. Trim the rough edges of
the dough, leaving about ¾ inch hanging over the
edge of the pan. Fold the excess dough under the edge
of the crust and finish the edges by pressing all
around with a fork or by pinching the dough between
your knuckle and two fingers.

To prepare the filling: Place the apples, sugar, flour,
cinnamon, and lemon juice in a large bowl and stir
until the sugar is fairly evenly distributed. Pour the
apples into the piecrust and press down slightly to
even them out and pack them down. Cut the butter into
8 pieces and place over the apples.

To prepare the topping: Place the topping ingredients
in a bowl and mix with a fork or your fingers until
crumbly.

Distribute the topping evenly over the apples. Place
the pie in the oven with a baking sheet on the rack
below it to catch any drippings. Bake for 50 to 60 minutes, or until the topping is golden brown.

✳ Kitchen Tip ✳

Because pies generally cook at a fairly high temperature,
the edges of the crust can get brown before the pie is
cooked in the center. Attaching 3-inch strips of aluminum
foil together to form a collar and placing it around the
edge of the crust when it is golden brown will prevent it
from browning any further.

This is a nice, light dessert that's great for hot summer days when berries are in season. I think the combination of strawberries and blueberries tastes great and looks cool together, but this pie can be made with any type of berries, or even peaches or nectarines.

M

FRESH BERRY PIE

SERVES 6

CRUST

¹/₃ cup butter

¹/₃ cup firmly packed brown sugar

1 cup flour

FILLING

2 pounds (8 cups) fresh strawberries

1 cup sugar

¹/₄ cup cornstarch

¹/₂ cup water

1 tablespoon lemon juice

¹/₂ pint (1 cup) fresh blueberries

To prepare the crust: Preheat the oven to 350°F.

Place the butter and brown sugar in a large bowl and mix with an electric mixer on medium speed for 2 minutes, or until fluffy. Add the flour and mix for 1 minute, or until just combined. Press the dough into the bottom and up the sides of an ungreased 9-inch pie pan. Bake for 15 minutes, or until the edges are lightly browned.

To prepare the filling: Remove the hulls from the strawberries. Crush enough of the strawberries to make 1 cup. Stir together the sugar and cornstarch in a large saucepan. Add the crushed strawberries and the ¹/₂ cup water to the pan and cook over medium heat, stirring occasionally, for 7 to 8 minutes, or until it comes to a boil. Stir in the lemon juice and let cool for 10 minutes. Add the whole strawberries and blueberries to the pan and stir to coat all of the fruit.

Pour the fruit into the crust and refrigerate for at least 2 hours, or until ready to serve.

KITCHEN MATH

We have included both volume and weight measurements for all of the berries to make it easier for you to figure out how much to buy. But not all cookbook writers are as nice as we are, so you really should know the following conversions:

    2 cups = 1 pint
    2 pints = 1 quart
    4 quarts = 1 gallon

That way, no matter how things are packaged, you will be able to figure out how much you need.

CINNAMON SWIRL CAKE

This is what we call a "sliver cake" in our house. Every time someone walks by, they take a little sliver, and pretty soon the whole cake is gone. The cream cheese makes it really moist, so it's easy to eat it with your hands. So if you make this cake for a specific purpose, you better hide it before that first cut gets made or it's a goner.

SERVES 10 TO 12

FILLING

¹/₄ cup butter

³/₄ cup flour

³/₄ cup firmly packed brown sugar

2 tablespoons ground cinnamon

CAKE

¹/₂ cup butter

8 ounces cream cheese

1¹/₄ cups sugar

2 eggs

1 teaspoon vanilla

¹/₂ cup milk

2 teaspoons baking powder

¹/₂ teaspoon salt

¹/₂ teaspoon baking soda

2 cups flour

To prepare the filling: Place the filling ingredients in a bowl and mix with a fork or your fingers until the mixture is completely combined and crumbly.

To prepare the cake: Preheat the oven to 350°F. Lightly butter or spray a tube or Bundt pan.

Place the butter, cream cheese, and sugar in a large bowl and mix with an electric mixer on low speed for 2 to 3 minutes, or until combined. Add the eggs and vanilla and mix on medium speed for 2 minutes, or until creamy. Add the milk and mix on low speed for 1 minute, or until smooth. Add the baking powder, salt, and baking soda and mix for 30 seconds. Add the flour and mix for 2 minutes, or until completely combined.

Pour one third of the cake batter into the prepared pan and sprinkle with half of the filling. Pour another third of the batter into the pan and sprinkle with the remaining filling. Pour the remaining batter into the pan and bake for 50 to 60 minutes, or until a toothpick inserted in the center comes out clean. Cool slightly and invert onto a serving platter.

This is another recipe I found when I was in Germany. It is one of my host father's favorite cakes. They made it for almost every birthday celebration while I was there. I always hoped there would be some left over, because then my host mom would serve it for tea the next day.

M

SPIRAL CAKE

SERVES 8 TO 10

CAKE

4 eggs

¼ cup water

⅔ cup sugar

½ cup flour

½ cup cornstarch

1 teaspoon baking powder

⅓ cup cocoa

TOPPINGS

¼ cup water

¼ cup sugar

1 tablespoon rum flavoring

2½ cups heavy cream

½ cup confectioners' sugar plus extra for dusting

1 pint (2 cups) fresh raspberries

To prepare the cake: Preheat the oven to 350°F. Line a 10 by 15-inch baking sheet with parchment paper.

Separate the eggs, placing the yolks in a large bowl and the whites in a medium bowl. Add the water to the egg yolks and beat with an electric mixer on medium speed for 1 minute, or until foamy. Add about two thirds of the sugar and mix for 2 minutes, or until light yellow and fluffy. Wash the beaters. Beat the egg whites on high speed for 2 minutes. Add the remaining sugar and beat for 2 more minutes, or until stiff peaks form. (When the beaters are lifted out of the egg whites, they form peaks that remain upright.)

Gently fold the egg whites into the egg yolks. Place the flour, cornstarch, baking powder, and cocoa into a sifter or sieve and sift into the eggs, stirring gently until just combined. Pour the batter onto the prepared baking sheet and bake for 20 minutes, or until the cake springs back when lightly pressed in the center. Remove the cake from the oven and cool completely.

To prepare the toppings: Place the water and sugar in a small saucepan and cook over medium-high heat for 3 minutes, or until it comes to a boil and the sugar is dissolved. Remove from the heat, cool slightly, and stir in the rum flavoring.

Place the cream in a large bowl and beat with an electric mixer on high speed for 3 to 4 minutes, or until stiff peaks form. (When the beaters are lifted out of the

KITCHEN SHORTCUT

Use 12 ounces of whipped topping and omit the heavy cream and confectioners' sugar, and the whipped cream preparation.

Kitchen Tip

While we don't generally tell you to wash your dishes, in this case it is critical to wash the beaters between mixing the egg yolks and egg whites. The protein and fat in the egg yolks will prevent the egg whites from whipping into stiff peaks. This is also why it is a good idea to separate egg yolks and whites one at a time into a small dish before adding them to the bowl. Even the smallest amount of egg yolk can keep the egg whites from whipping up.

cream, they form peaks that remain upright.) Add the confectioners' sugar and beat on low speed for 30 seconds, or until just combined. Refrigerate until ready to use.

To assemble the cake: Place a clean towel on a flat surface and sprinkle with confectioners' sugar. Turn the cooled cake out onto the towel and remove the parchment paper. Brush the rum flavoring mixture on the cake. Arrange most of the raspberries on top of the cake, reserving a few for garnish. Spread two thirds of the whipped cream onto the cake. Cut the cake lengthwise into 6 equal-width strips. Roll one of the cake strips into a spiral with the whipped cream side in and place the spiral flat in the center of a serving platter. Continue the spiral with the remaining cake strips, forming one large spiral. Decorate with the remaining whipped cream and berries.

This super sweet dessert is beyond good. We thought it would be fun to spruce up good old pecan pie—and what could be better than adding chocolate. I love to eat this warm with vanilla ice cream or whipped cream.

CHOCOLATE CHIP-PECAN PIE

SERVES 8

CRUST

1 cup flour

¹/₂ teaspoon salt

¹/₃ cup cold butter or shortening

3 tablespoons water

KITCHEN SHORTCUT

Use 1 prepared piecrust and omit the crust ingredients and preparation.

To prepare the crust: Preheat the oven to 350°F.

Stir together the flour and salt in a large bowl. Add the butter and cut in with a pastry cutter or two knives until the mixture is the size of small peas. Add the water and blend gently with a fork until the dough just starts to hold together. (If you prefer to use a food processor, place the flour, salt, and butter in the bowl of a food processor and pulse for about 10 seconds, or until crumbly. Drizzle the water into the food processor while pulsing until the dough just forms a ball.) Form the dough into a ¹/₂-inch-thick disk and place on a lightly floured work surface. Roll the dough into a 10-inch circle. Fold the dough in half and transfer to an ungreased 8-inch pie pan. Gently unfold the dough and press it into the pan, patting out any air pockets. Trim the rough edges of the dough, leaving about ³/₄ inch hanging over the edge of the pan. Fold the excess dough under the edge of the crust and finish the edges by pressing all around with a fork or by pinching the dough between your knuckle and two fingers.

FILLING

1 cup pecan halves

3 eggs

1 cup sugar

$^1/_2$ cup light corn syrup

5 tablespoons butter, melted

1 teaspoon vanilla

$^1/_2$ teaspoon salt

$^1/_2$ cup chocolate chips

To prepare the filling: Spread the pecans on a baking sheet and toast in the oven for 10 minutes, or until lightly browned.

Place the eggs in a large bowl and beat well. Add the sugar, corn syrup, butter, vanilla, salt, and chocolate chips and stir until completely combined. Pour the mixture into the piecrust and arrange the pecan halves on top.

Bake for 50 to 55 minutes, or until the center is set. (The center will puff up during cooking and fall as the pie cools.) Cool completely before serving.

Custards, Puddings, and Stuff

We had chocolate éclairs a lot when I was growing up, partially because we really liked them and partially because we always had the ingredients in the house. Feel free to borrow my trick for making these: "Mom, you make the best chocolate éclairs ever." Works every time (okay, it works occasionally). But hey, when it works, it's what I call a perfect balance: good food and no work.

CHOCOLATE ÉCLAIRS

MAKES 12 ÉCLAIRS

FILLING

3/4 cup sugar

1/4 cup cornstarch

Pinch of salt

3 cups milk

3 egg yolks

2 teaspoons vanilla

2 tablespoons butter

SHELLS

1/2 cup butter

1 cup hot water

1 cup flour

1/2 teaspoon salt

4 eggs

FROSTING

1 ounce unsweetened chocolate

1/4 cup butter

1 cup confectioners' sugar

1 tablespoon milk

To prepare the filling: Fill a large bowl about halfway with ice cubes and add enough water to almost cover the ice.

Combine the sugar, cornstarch, and salt in a saucepan. Gradually stir in the milk. Cook over medium-high heat, stirring frequently, for 10 minutes, or until the mixture comes to a boil. Boil for 1 minute. Beat the egg yolks slightly in a small bowl. Very slowly whisk some of the hot liquid into the eggs to temper them. Pour the eggs into the pan and cook over low heat, stirring constantly, for 1 minute, or until the mixture barely begins to bubble. (Do not allow the mixture to boil or the eggs will curdle.) Remove the pan from the heat and stir in the vanilla and butter. Strain the filling into a bowl through a fine-mesh sieve and place the bowl in the ice water bath. Stir occasionally for 20 to 30 minutes, or until cool. Remove the bowl from the ice water bath, lay a piece of plastic wrap right on the filling, and refrigerate for 1 hour, or until cold.

To prepare the shells: Preheat the oven to 425°F.

Place the butter and water in a saucepan and cook over medium heat for 5 minutes, or until it comes to a boil. Add the flour and salt all at once and cook, stirring constantly, for 1 minute, or until the mixture pulls away from the sides of the pan. Remove from the heat and add the eggs one at a time, stirring until each egg is completely incorporated. Spread the batter on an ungreased baking sheet in twelve 1 by 3-inch rectangles and bake for 30 to 35 minutes, or until golden brown. Turn off the oven. Poke a hole in one end of each éclair shell with a knife and let them dry in the oven for 20 minutes.

To prepare the frosting: Place the chocolate in a small microwave-safe bowl and microwave on high heat for 1 minute, then stir. If the chocolate is not all melted, place it back in the microwave for 15 seconds at a time, stirring after each time, until it is completely melted. Be careful not to let the chocolate start to bubble or it will burn and get gritty. Add the butter, confectioners' sugar, and milk and stir until smooth.

To assemble the éclairs: Place the cold filling in a pastry bag. Insert the tip into each éclair shell and squeeze in some of the filling. Spread some of the frosting over the top of each éclair and refrigerate until ready to serve.

My Great-Grandma Goebel made dessert for her family every day, and with ten kids, that's no small feat. They lived on a farm, so they had plenty of eggs and milk, making pudding a logical choice. We make this dessert with lemon pudding, but my grandma remembers having it with vanilla or chocolate pudding.

M

FLOATING ISLAND PUDDING

SERVES 4

MERINGUE

2 egg whites

1/2 teaspoon cream of tartar

2 tablespoons sugar

PUDDING

3/4 cup sugar

1 1/2 tablespoons cornstarch

1/4 teaspoon salt

1 1/4 cups water

2 egg yolks

1 tablespoon butter

1/3 cup lemon juice

To prepare the meringue: Preheat the oven to 375°F.

Place the egg whites and cream of tartar in a bowl and beat with an electric mixer on high speed for 2 minutes, or until soft peaks form. (When the beaters are lifted out of the cream, they form peaks that fold over when the beaters pull away.) Add the sugar and beat for 1 minute, or until thick and glossy. Form 4 mounds of meringue in an ungreased 8- or 9-inch shallow baking dish and bake for 10 to 12 minutes, or until golden brown on the edges.

To prepare the pudding: Place the sugar, cornstarch, salt, and water in a small saucepan and cook over medium-high heat, stirring frequently, for 5 minutes, or until it begins to boil. Boil for 1 minute. Place the egg yolks in a small bowl and beat slightly. Very slowly

KITCHEN CHEMISTRY

Cream of tartar always seems to get added to egg whites, but I never really knew why. I did a little research and found out that it actually serves two purposes. Cream of tartar, or potassium bitartrate if you care, is an acid that serves as an interfering agent to stabilize the egg proteins and keep sucrose molecules liquid. In plain English, it stabilizes the eggs and keeps the sugar from crystallizing.

whisk some of the hot mixture into the eggs to temper them. Pour the eggs into the pan and cook over low heat, stirring constantly, for 1 minute, or until the mixture barely begins to bubble. (Do not allow the pudding to boil or the eggs will curdle.) Remove the pan from the heat and stir in the butter and lemon juice.

Carefully pour the pudding around the meringues. The meringues may loosen on their own and pop to the top of the pudding. If they do not, carefully run a knife or spatula around them to loosen them. Refrigerate for at least 1 hour, or until ready to serve.

This dish is best made with day-old croissants, so if yours are fresh, pop them in the oven for a few minutes to dry them out. If you are making this for your family, put it in a casserole as we did here, but if you are making it for guests, it looks cooler in individual custard dishes.

RASPBERRY-CROISSANT BREAD PUDDING WITH VANILLA SAUCE

SERVES 6

PUDDING

4 eggs

2/3 cup sugar

1 teaspoon vanilla

2 cups milk

1/2 teaspoon salt

6 croissants

1/2 pint (1 cup) fresh or
   frozen raspberries

SAUCE

1 cup heavy cream

2 egg yolks

2 tablespoons sugar

2 teaspoons vanilla

To prepare the pudding: Preheat the oven to 350°F. Lightly butter or spray a 2-quart casserole.

Whisk together the eggs and sugar in a large bowl. Add the vanilla, milk, and salt and mix well. Cut the croissants into 1/2- to 3/4-inch cubes and stir into the egg mixture. Gently stir in the raspberries and pour the mixture into the casserole. Place the casserole in a larger baking pan. Place the pans in the oven and carefully pour in enough hot water to come 1 inch up the sides of the casserole. Bake for 55 to 65 minutes, or until the pudding is set in the middle.

To prepare the sauce: Place the cream in a small saucepan over medium-high heat and bring to a boil. Whisk together the egg yolks and sugar in a small bowl. Very slowly whisk some of the hot liquid into the eggs to temper them. Pour the eggs into the saucepan and cook over low heat, stirring constantly, for 2 minutes, or until the mixture coats the back of a metal spoon. (Do not allow the sauce to boil or the eggs will curdle.) Remove the pan from the heat, stir in the vanilla, and strain through a fine-mesh sieve. The sauce can be served warm or cold.

Place some of the warm pudding in the center of each plate and spoon the sauce over the pudding.

This was my Great-Grandma Goebel's signature dessert. Anytime she went to a potluck dinner she would bring this, and with good reason. It's really good and different from any other dessert I've ever seen. The recipe seems like it has a lot of steps, but if you think of stirring constantly as stirring most of the time, you can get the other steps done while the custard is cooking.

POPPY SEED TORTE

SERVES 12

CRUST

1 cup graham cracker
    crumbs

1 cup flour

1/2 cup butter, melted

1/2 cup ground walnuts

FILLING

5 eggs

2 cups milk

1 1/2 cups sugar

1/4 cup poppy seeds

1/4 teaspoon salt

2 tablespoons cornstarch

1 1/2 tablespoons (2 packets)
    powdered gelatin

1/2 cup water

1/2 teaspoon cream of tartar

TOPPING

1 cup heavy cream

1/4 cup confectioners' sugar

To prepare the crust: Preheat the oven to 350°F.

Stir together the crust ingredients in an ungreased 9 by 13-inch pan and pat firmly into the bottom of the pan. Bake for 15 minutes.

To prepare the filling: Separate the eggs, placing the yolks in a large saucepan and the whites in a large bowl. Add the milk and 1 cup of the sugar to the saucepan and cook over medium heat, stirring constantly, for 5 minutes, or until the sugar is dissolved. Add the poppy seeds, salt, and cornstarch and cook, stirring constantly, for 7 to 8 minutes, or until it just begins to bubble and is thick. (Do not allow the mixture to boil or the eggs will curdle.) Remove the pan from the heat.

Combine the gelatin and water and let stand for 5 minutes, or until the gelatin is dissolved. Stir the gelatin into the warm egg yolk mixture.

Add the cream of tartar to the egg whites and beat with an electric mixer on high speed for 2 minutes. Add the remaining 1/2 cup sugar and beat for 2 minutes, or until stiff peaks form. (When the beaters are lifted out of the egg whites, they form peaks that remain upright.) Gently fold the egg whites into the custard. Carefully pour the filling over the crust and refrigerate for at least 2 hours.

KITCHEN SHORTCUT
Use 8 ounces of whipped topping and omit the topping ingredients and preparation.

To prepare the topping: Place the cream in a bowl and beat with an electric mixer on high speed for 3 minutes, or until soft peaks form. (When the beaters are lifted out of the cream, they form peaks that fold over when the beaters pull away.) Add the confectioners' sugar and beat until combined.

Spread the whipped cream over the filling and refrigerate the torte until ready to serve.

Kitchen Vocab

The process of dissolving gelatin in water is called **blooming** the gelatin. This is necessary to activate the gelatin. If you were to pour it in dry, it would just get lumpy and would not make the custard gel.

M

I call this the "international dessert." I got this recipe from my German host sister, which makes it an Italian dessert made from a German recipe by an American. But no matter who came up with it, it's good. This recipe does contain uncooked eggs, so be careful about serving it to small children, the elderly, or anyone who has a weakened immune system.

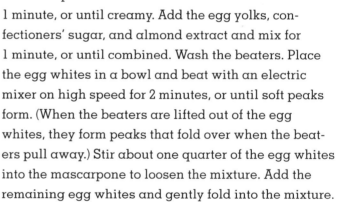

TIRAMISU

SERVES 9

16 ounces mascarpone cheese

4 egg yolks

1 cup confectioners' sugar

1/2 teaspoon almond extract

2 egg whites

1 (5.25-ounce) box ladyfingers

1/2 cup strong brewed coffee

Cocoa for dusting

** Kitchen Tip

Mascarpone is a soft, triple-cream cheese that can be expensive and difficult to find. If you can't find it or don't want to pay the asking price, combine 16 ounces of cream cheese with 1/2 cup of whipping cream for a good substitution.

Place the mascarpone in a bowl and beat with an electric mixer on medium speed for 1 minute, or until creamy. Add the egg yolks, confectioners' sugar, and almond extract and mix for 1 minute, or until combined. Wash the beaters. Place the egg whites in a bowl and beat with an electric mixer on high speed for 2 minutes, or until soft peaks form. (When the beaters are lifted out of the egg whites, they form peaks that fold over when the beaters pull away.) Stir about one quarter of the egg whites into the mascarpone to loosen the mixture. Add the remaining egg whites and gently fold into the mixture.

Arrange half of the ladyfingers in the bottom of an ungreased 9-inch square pan and brush with half of the coffee. Spoon half of the mascarpone mixture evenly over the ladyfingers. Repeat the layers with the remaining ingredients and sprinkle the top with the cocoa. Refrigerate for at least 2 hours before serving.

KITCHEN HISTORY

Tiramisu means "pick-me-up" in Italian. It was named that for the high energy content of the eggs, sugar, and coffee. It is a fairly recent concoction having been created in the early 1970s at Le Beccherie restaurant in Treviso, Italy.

CHOCOLATE CRÈME BRÛLÉE

M

This dessert caused quite an argument in our house. I made half of the batch with white chocolate and half with semisweet. I loved the white chocolate. Everyone else liked the semisweet. After about a week of going back and forth about it, I finally gave in. So the recipe here is with semisweet chocolate, but I still say it's better with white.

SERVES 4

Kitchen Vocab

Custards are usually cooked in a pan of water called a **water bath**. The water bath gently cooks the custard and keeps the eggs from curdling. Without the water bath, the eggs will cook too quickly and you will end up with scrambled eggs. Not good.

½ cup half-and-half

4 egg yolks

⅓ cup sugar plus extra for dusting

½ cup chocolate chips

1½ cups heavy cream

Preheat the oven to 325°F.

Place the half-and-half in a small saucepan and cook over medium-high heat for 5 minutes, or until it comes to a boil.

Whisk together the egg yolks and sugar in a medium bowl. Very slowly pour the hot half-and-half into the eggs to temper them, whisking constantly. Add the chocolate chips and whisk until they are melted. Whisk in the cream and strain through a fine-mesh sieve.

Pour the custard into 4 ungreased ramekins or crème brûlée dishes and place them in a baking pan. Put the baking pan in the oven and carefully add 1 inch of hot water to create a water bath. Bake for 35 minutes, or until the edges are set and the middle is slightly jiggly.

Cool slightly and refrigerate until ready to serve.

Evenly coat the top of each crème brûlée with a thin layer of sugar and, using a kitchen torch or placing the crème brûlées under a gas broiler, melt the sugar until it is golden brown and caramelized.

M

This is another one of those international desserts. I got the recipe from a friend in France who got it out of a magazine from England. I fell in love with it after making it with fresh cherries from my French friend's tree. I usually make this eggy custard with peaches or apricots, but this super easy dessert is good with almost any type of fruit.

PEACH CLAFoUTI

SERVES 8

i4 eggs

½ cup flour

⅔ cup sugar

1½ cups milk

1 teaspoon vanilla

¼ cup butter, melted

1 (29-ounce) can peach halves

Preheat the oven to 350°F. Lightly butter or spray a 10-inch quiche or cake pan.

Place the eggs in a large bowl and beat slightly. Add the flour and stir until combined. Add the sugar and stir until smooth. Add the milk, vanilla, and butter and stir until melted. Drain the peaches and arrange them round side up in the bottom of the prepared pan. Pour the batter over the peaches and bake for 45 minutes, or until set in the middle. (It will puff up during baking and fall as it cools.) Cool slightly and serve warm or refrigerate until ready to serve.

Kitchen Vocab

Clafouti (kla-foo-TEE) is a French country dessert traditionally made by topping fresh fruit with batter. Sometimes the batter is more custard-like, as ours is, and sometimes it is more cake-like.

GINGER CRÈME CARAMEL

This is one of those impressive desserts that is really easy to make. The most difficult part is getting the caramel all around the inside of the custard cup. Cooking this in a water bath helps to keep the eggs from scrambling, so you end up with a really smooth custard with just a hint of ginger.

SERVES 4

CARAMEL

¹/₂ cup sugar

¹/₄ cup water

CUSTARD

1¹/₂ cups milk

1 2-inch piece fresh ginger

3 eggs

¹/₂ cup sugar

Pinch of salt

To prepare the caramel: Place the sugar in a small saucepan and pour in the water, making sure all of the sugar gets wet. Cook over medium-high heat, without stirring, for 10 minutes, or until the sugar turns deep golden brown. Immediately pour the caramel into 4 small ramekins or custard cups and swirl it around to coat the sides and bottom of the dishes.

To prepare the custard: Preheat the oven to 325°F.

Place the milk in a small saucepan. Cut the ginger in thin slices and add to the milk. (The ginger does not need to be peeled because it will be removed later.)

Cook the milk over medium-high heat for 5 minutes, or until it just begins to steam. Remove the pan from the heat and let the ginger steep for 10 minutes. Return the pan to the heat and cook for 5 minutes, or until it just begins to steam. Do not allow the milk to boil.

Whisk together the eggs, sugar, and salt in a bowl and slowly whisk in the hot milk. Strain the custard through a fine-mesh sieve and pour it into the custard cups. Place the cups in a baking pan, put the baking pan in the oven, and add 1 inch of hot water to create a water bath. Bake for 50 to 60 minutes, or until just set in the center. Refrigerate for 3 hours before serving.

When we were little, pudding pops were one of our favorite things to eat and then they stopped making them. We didn't even think about the fact that we could make them ourselves until we were coming up with ideas for this book and thinking about all the desserts we loved. All those years of pudding pop eating lost . . . that's sad.

PUDDING POPS

MAKES 8 PUDDING POPS

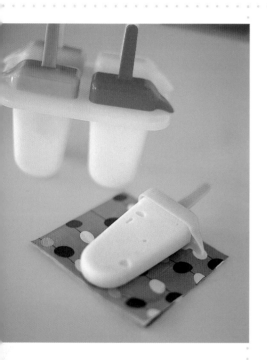

Fill a large bowl about halfway with ice cubes and add enough water to almost cover the ice.

Combine the sugar, cornstarch, and salt in a saucepan. Gradually add the milk. Cook over medium-high heat, stirring frequently, for 5 minutes, or until the mixture comes to a boil. Boil for 1 minute. Beat the eggs in a small bowl. Very slowly whisk some of the hot liquid into the eggs to temper them. Pour the eggs into the pan and cook over low heat, stirring constantly, for 1 minute, or until the mixture barely begins to bubble. (Do not allow the pudding to boil or the eggs will curdle.) Remove the pan from the heat and stir in the vanilla.

1 cup sugar

1/4 cup cornstarch

Pinch of salt

4 cups milk

4 eggs

2 teaspoons vanilla

8 craft sticks

kitchen safety

When cooking perishable foods, such as eggs and milk, it is important to keep them below 40°F or above 140°F as much as possible. Ice water baths decrease the time that the food is in the danger zone between 41°F and 139°F, when bacteria growth can happen. So even though it may seem like a pain, giving your family food poisoning would be worse. You'd never hear the end of that one.

Strain the pudding into a bowl through a fine-mesh sieve and place the bowl in the ice water bath. Stir occasionally for 20 to 30 minutes, or until the pudding is cool. Refrigerate for 1 hour, or until completely chilled. Freeze in an ice cream maker according to the manufacturer's directions. Spoon the frozen pudding into Popsicle molds or small plastic cups with craft sticks, and freeze completely.

I realize that it seems like it would be hard to burn chocolate in a microwave, but really pay attention to the directions. The last time I made this I burned the chocolate twice because I was too impatient to do it correctly. Needless to say, my mom was not pleased. The good news is the mousse was really good when I got the chocolate right.

CHOCOLATE-ALMOND MOUSSE

SERVES 6

18 almonds, for garnish

1 cup chocolate chips

1 egg

2 egg yolks

Pinch of salt

6 tablespoons sugar

1 teaspoon almond extract

1 tablespoon water

1 cup heavy cream

Preheat the oven to 350°F.

Place the almonds on a baking sheet and toast in the oven for 10 minutes, or until lightly browned.

Place the chocolate in a small microwave-safe bowl and microwave on high heat for 1 minute, then stir. If the chocolate is not all melted, place it back in the microwave for 15 seconds at a time, stirring after each time, until it is completely melted. Be careful not to let the chocolate start to bubble or it will burn and get gritty.

Fill the bottom of a double boiler about halfway with water and bring to a simmer over medium heat. Remove the top pan of the double boiler from the heat and place the egg, egg yolks, and salt in it. Beat the eggs with an electric mixer for 1 minute, or until foamy. Slowly add the sugar while continuing to beat. Add the almond extract and water and beat for 30 seconds, or until combined. Place the pan on top of the double boiler and cook, whisking constantly, for 4 to 5 minutes, or until pale yellow and fluffy. Remove the top pan of the double boiler from the heat again and beat the mixture with an electric mixer on high speed for 5 minutes, or until thick enough to fold over on itself and hold its shape for a few seconds. Whisk some of the

egg mixture into the chocolate to loosen it up, then whisk the melted chocolate into the eggs.

Place the cream in a bowl and beat with an electric mixer on medium-high speed for 3 minutes, or until soft peaks form. (When the beaters are lifted out of the cream, they form peaks that fold over when the beaters pull away.) Gently fold the cream into the chocolate mixture until thoroughly combined, then spoon into 6 serving dishes. Arrange 3 almonds on top of each dish and refrigerate for at least 2 hours before serving.

Holiday Stuff

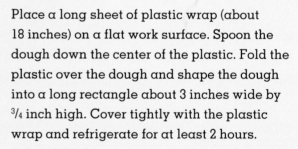

These are my favorite cookies ever. They are so buttery that they dissolve in your mouth. Whenever I get Christmas food coma, I just remember that I've probably eaten about a thousand of them. (Okay, maybe not a thousand, but a lot.)

CHOCOLATE-DIPPED SHORTBREAD

MAKES ABOUT 4 DOZEN COOKIES

SHORTBREAD

1 cup butter

$^1/_2$ cup confectioners' sugar

2 teaspoons vanilla

$2^1/_2$ cups cake flour

To prepare the shortbread: Place the butter and confectioners' sugar in a large bowl and mix with an electric mixer on low speed for 1 minute, or until combined. Add the vanilla and mix for 2 minutes, or until fluffy. Add the flour and mix for 2 minutes, or until completely incorporated.

Place a long sheet of plastic wrap (about 18 inches) on a flat work surface. Spoon the dough down the center of the plastic. Fold the plastic over the dough and shape the dough into a long rectangle about 3 inches wide by $^3/_4$ inch high. Cover tightly with the plastic wrap and refrigerate for at least 2 hours.

Preheat the oven to 350°F.

Remove the dough from the refrigerator and remove the plastic wrap. Cut the dough into $^1/_4$-inch-thick slices and place about $^1/_2$ inch apart on an ungreased baking sheet. Bake for 18 to 20 minutes, or until they just begin to brown on the edges. Remove the cookies from the pan and cool on parchment or waxed paper.

CHOCOLATE

1 cup chocolate chips

⅔ cup chopped nuts or sprinkles

Kitchen Vocab

Cake flour is a finely textured flour that is often used in baking to give a lighter, more delicate texture to cakes and pastries. We don't use it that often, but in this case it makes the cookies much lighter than if you use regular flour.

To prepare the chocolate: Place the chocolate chips in a small microwave-safe bowl and microwave on high for 1 minute, then stir. If the chocolate is not all melted, place it back in the microwave for 15 seconds at a time, stirring after each time, until it is completely melted. Be careful not to let the chocolate start to bubble or it will burn and get gritty.

Line 2 baking sheets with parchment or waxed paper. Dip one end of each cooled cookie into the melted chocolate, scraping the bottom of the cookie on the edge of the bowl to remove any excess chocolate. (If you don't scrape off the bottoms, the chocolate spreads and they end up looking like chocolate lollipops.) Immediately dip the chocolate part of the cookie into the nuts or sprinkles. Place the cookies on the prepared baking sheets and refrigerate for 10 minutes, or until the chocolate is set.

KITCHEN HISTORY

Shortbread originated in northern Europe, but because it contained butter it was only eaten by the lower classes. Since butter was a by-product of farming, it was considered the food of the poor. The middle classes didn't start using it until the late fifteenth century, and the nobility wouldn't touch it until the mid-sixteenth century. Times certainly have changed.

These are super tasty cookies! I am normally not fond of crispy cookies, but these just melt in your mouth, so I make an exception. When we make these at Christmastime, we use green and red sprinkles, but any other time of year we use the chocolate or multicolored ones.

OATMEAL REFRIGERATOR COOKIES

MAKES ABOUT 5 DOZEN COOKIES

1 cup butter

1 cup confectioners' sugar

2 tablespoons vanilla

1½ cups flour

1 teaspoon baking soda

1 cup rolled oats

3 bottles sprinkles

Place the butter in a large bowl and beat with an electric mixer on high speed for 1 minute, or until creamy. Add the confectioners' sugar and vanilla and mix on medium speed for 2 minutes, or until light and fluffy. Gradually add in the flour and baking soda and mix for 1 minute, or until smooth. Add the oatmeal and mix for 1 minute, or until completely combined. Refrigerate the dough for 10 minutes for easier handling.

Divide the dough into 3 equal pieces. Roll each piece into a 1½-inch-diameter log. Pour the sprinkles onto a baking pan and roll each of the logs in the sprinkles. Wrap each log in plastic wrap and refrigerate for at least 3 hours.

Preheat the oven to 325°F.

Cut the logs into ¼-inch-thick slices and place them about 2 inches apart on an ungreased baking sheet. Bake the cookies for 20 minutes, or until they are lightly browned. Remove them from the pan and cool on parchment or waxed paper.

Kitchen Vocab

Confectioners' sugar is just powdered sugar. It got its official name because it was commonly used in candy making and baking at confectionary shops. But it is usually called powdered sugar because it is . . . well, powdered.

CiNNAMoN BuTToNS

These are one of my mom's favorite Christmas cookies. They are really delicate cinnamon cookies with just a hint of almond flavor. We always make them with a small scoop because it is easier than rolling them all and they all end up the same size.

MAKES ABOUT 5 DOZEN COOKIES

1 cup butter

1 cup ground almonds

⅓ cup sugar

1⅔ cups flour

¼ cup superfine sugar

2 teaspoons ground cinnamon

Kitchen Tip

You can buy superfine sugar in any grocery store. But if you are like us and never plan that far ahead, you can make it by putting regular granulated sugar in a blender or food processor and pulsing it until it is fairly fine. Just be careful not to pulse it for too long or you will end up with powdered sugar.

Place the butter, almonds, and sugar in a large bowl and beat with an electric mixer on medium speed for 1 minute, or until light and fluffy. Add the flour and mix for 2 minutes, or until completely incorporated. Cover the dough with plastic wrap and refrigerate for at least 2 hours.

Preheat the oven to 325°F.

Place the superfine sugar and cinnamon in a shallow bowl and mix well.

Scoop or roll the cookies into ¾-inch balls and place them about 1 inch apart on an ungreased baking sheet. Bake for 20 minutes, or until they just start to brown on the edges. Cool for about 5 minutes on the pan, then roll them in the cinnamon sugar. Cool on parchment or waxed paper.

M

These are a mix between kolaches (Polish sweet buns) and thumbprint cookies. We took the cream-cheese dough from the kolaches and the jelly in the center of thumbprints and made a cute little cookie that looks like a flower and is much easier than rolling out kolaches. You can use whatever jam you like, but we like raspberry the best.

SNOWFLAKE COOKIES

MAKES ABOUT 9 DOZEN COOKIES

1 cup butter

4 ounces cream cheese

1 cup sugar

1 egg yolk

1/2 teaspoon vanilla

2 1/2 cups flour

1/3 cup raspberry jam

Confectioners' sugar for dusting

Preheat the oven to 350°F.

Place the butter and cream cheese in a large bowl and beat with an electric mixer on low speed for 2 minutes, or until smooth. Add the sugar, egg yolk, and vanilla and mix on medium speed for 2 minutes, or until fluffy. Add the flour and mix on low speed for 1 minute, or until completely combined.

Place some of the dough into a cookie press fitted with a flower design and press the cookies onto an ungreased baking sheet. (If you don't have a cookie press, roll the dough into 3/4-inch balls.) Press down the center of each cookie slightly with your finger and bake for 6 minutes. Remove the pan from the oven and spoon a small amount of raspberry jam into the center of each cookie. (Be careful not to add too much jam or it will run over the edges of the cookie while baking.) Return the pan to the oven and cook for 8 to 10 minutes, or until the cookies are set and the edges just begin to brown. Place the cookies on parchment or waxed paper and sprinkle with the confectioners' sugar.

* Kitchen Tip *

Crunchy cookies versus soft is always an argument in our house. Jill and I like soft cookies and our parents prefer them crunchy. The good news is, with a couple of little variations you can accommodate everyone. For soft cookies, bake them for a shorter time and cool them on waxed or parchment paper on a flat surface. For crunchy cookies, bake them a little longer and cool them on wire racks.

These are my cousin's favorite of our Christmas cookies, except he calls them buckeyes. These can be tedious to make with all of the scooping and dipping, but we like them so much we think they're worth it.

PEANUT BUTTER BALLS

MAKES ABOUT 9 DOZEN PEANUT BUTTER BALLS

2 cups peanut butter

¹/₂ cup butter

4 cups confectioners' sugar

3 cups crispy rice cereal

4 cups chocolate chips

Place the peanut butter and butter in a large microwave-safe bowl and microwave on high for 1 minute, or until the butter is melted. Stir until the butter is completely incorporated into the peanut butter. Add the confectioners' sugar and stir until combined. Add the crispy rice cereal and stir until evenly distributed. (The mixture will be dry.) Using a small scoop or your hands, press the mixture into 1-inch balls.

Place the chocolate chips in a microwave-safe bowl and microwave on high heat for 2 minutes, and then stir. If they are not all melted, place them back in the microwave for 15 seconds at a time, stirring after each time, until they are completely melted. Be careful not to let the chocolate start to bubble or it will burn and get gritty.

Line 2 baking sheets with parchment or waxed paper. Lower 1 of the balls into the chocolate and use a fork to gently roll it around until it is

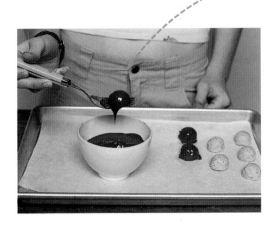

completely coated. Lift the peanut butter ball from the chocolate with the fork and hold it above the chocolate to allow the excess chocolate to drip back into the bowl. Scrape the chocolate from the bottom of the fork and place the peanut butter ball on one of the prepared baking sheets. Repeat with the remaining balls. Refrigerate for 10 minutes, or until the chocolate is set.

✳ Kitchen Tip ✳

In a professional kitchen, chocolate used for dipping is always tempered. Tempering the chocolate allows it to form a firm shell that will not melt when you hold it. Because it is a tedious process, we generally only temper chocolate when we are giving candy as gifts. To temper chocolate, place the chopped chocolate or chocolate chips in a double boiler over barely simmering water. Heat the chocolate to 115°F. Remove the chocolate from the heat and stir continuously until it cools to 80°F. Then reheat the chocolate in the double boiler to 85°F. Now the chocolate is ready for dipping.

The Yule log, or bûche de Noël, is a traditional French cake that represents the old custom of placing a huge log covered in oil and wine in the fireplace on Christmas Eve. (Can you say *combustible*?) Since we aren't fond of the cream filling in the traditional version, we modified the recipe to a German chocolate cake with a coconut-pecan filling, but we still make it in the traditional log shape.

YULE LOG

SERVES 8 TO 10

CAKE

2 ounces German chocolate

¼ cup boiling water

1½ teaspoons white wine vinegar

½ cup milk

2 eggs

½ cup butter

1 cup sugar

½ teaspoon vanilla

¼ teaspoon salt

½ teaspoon baking soda

1¼ cups flour

To prepare the cake: Preheat the oven to 350°F. Line an 11 by 17-inch baking sheet with parchment paper and lightly batter or spray the parchment.

Place the chocolate in a small bowl, pour the boiling water over the chocolate, and stir occasionally until the chocolate is completely melted.

Place the vinegar in a liquid measuring cup and add enough milk to make ½ cup.

Separate the eggs, reserving the yolks to use later in this recipe. Place the egg whites in a large bowl and beat with an electric mixer on high speed for 3 minutes, or until stiff peaks form. (When the beaters are lifted out of the egg whites, they form peaks that remain upright.)

Place the butter and sugar in a large bowl and beat with an electric mixer on medium speed for 2 minutes, or until fluffy. Add the egg yolks one at a time, beating well after each addition. Add the melted chocolate and vanilla and mix until completely combined. Add the salt and baking soda and mix for 30 seconds. Mixing on low speed, alternately add half of the flour and milk at a time, beating until smooth after each addition. Gently fold in the egg whites. Pour the batter onto the prepared baking sheet and bake for 20 minutes, or until the cake springs back when lightly pressed in the center. Cool for 5 minutes.

[continued]

FILLING

1 cup evaporated milk

1 cup sugar

3 egg yolks

1/2 cup butter

1 teaspoon vanilla

1/3 cup coconut

1 cup chopped pecans

FROSTING

4 ounces unsweetened
    chocolate

3/4 cup butter

3 cups confectioners' sugar

1 teaspoon vanilla

1 1/2 tablespoons milk

Pinch of salt

To prepare the filling: Place the evaporated milk, sugar, egg yolks, and butter in a saucepan and cook over medium-high heat for 10 minutes, or until thick. Stir in the vanilla, coconut, and pecans and stir until thick enough to spread.

To assemble the cake: Place a 20-inch piece of plastic wrap on a flat surface. Invert the warm cake onto the plastic and remove the parchment paper. Spread the filling evenly over the entire cake. Starting on a 10-inch side, carefully roll the cake into a spiral, using the plastic wrap to help keep it as tight as possible. Wrap the roll tightly in the plastic wrap and let cool completely.

To prepare the frosting: Place the chocolate in a small microwave-safe bowl and microwave on high heat for 1 minute, then stir. If the chocolate is not all melted, place it back in the microwave for 15 seconds at a time, stirring after each time, until it is completely melted. Be careful not to let the chocolate start to bubble or it will burn and get gritty.

Place the butter in a large bowl and beat with an electric mixer on medium speed for 1 minute, or until fluffy. Add the confectioners' sugar and melted chocolate and mix for 1 minute, or until even in color. Add the vanilla, milk, and salt and mix for 2 minutes, or until fluffy.

To assemble the Yule log: Place the rolled cake on a serving platter seam side down. Spread the frosting over the entire cake as smoothly as possible. Using the tines of a fork, scrape down the length of the cake to simulate bark. Using a skewer or toothpick, scrape tight spirals on the ends of the cake to simulate tree rings.

KITCHEN HISTORY

German chocolate cake is actually an American creation that was named for the German chocolate in the recipe. And no, the German chocolate isn't from Germany either. German chocolate is a sweetened baker's chocolate that is closer in flavor to milk chocolate than to unsweetened baking chocolate. It was developed for Baker's Chocolate Company in 1852 by an Englishman named . . . you got it, Sam German. Mystery solved.

Trifle is a layered dessert made with cake, fruit, and cream. It is a long-standing holiday tradition in England. They also call this Tipsy Cake, Tipsy Pudding, Tipsy Squire, or Tipsy Parson, probably because of the amount of sherry in the original version. We skipped the sherry and made ours with gingerbread, pumpkin cream, and a few pecans to add a little crunch.

GINGERBREAD AND PUMPKIN TRIFLE

SERVES 8 TO 10

CAKE

1 1/2 teaspoons white wine vinegar

1/2 cup milk

1 egg

1/2 cup light molasses

1/4 cup butter, melted

1/4 cup sugar

1 teaspoon baking powder

1/4 teaspoon baking soda

1/4 teaspoon salt

1/4 teaspoon ground cloves

2 teaspoons ground ginger

1 teaspoon ground cinnamon

1 1/2 cups flour

To prepare the cake: Preheat the oven to 350°F. Lightly butter or spray an 8-inch square pan.

Place the vinegar in a liquid measuring cup and add enough milk to make 1/2 cup.

Place the egg in a large bowl and beat well with a fork. Add the milk, molasses, and butter and mix well. Add the sugar, baking powder, baking soda, salt, cloves, ginger, and cinnamon and mix well. Add the flour and stir until just combined. Pour the batter into the prepared pan and bake 25 to 30 minutes, or until

1 cup pecan halves

1½ cups heavy cream

1 cup confectioners' sugar

2 teaspoons ground cinnamon plus extra for dusting

1 teaspoon ground cloves

1 teaspoon ground ginger

1 (15-ounce) can pumpkin purée

* *
Kitchen Tip

You may notice that several of our recipes use a combination of vinegar and milk. This is our substitution for buttermilk. We never have buttermilk in the house and are way too lazy to make a trip to the store just for that, so we use this substitution all the time. For each cup of buttermilk, use 1 tablespoon of vinegar and add enough milk to make 1 cup. Works perfectly every time.

the cake springs back when pressed gently in the center. Remove from the oven and cool completely. Leave the oven on at 350°F.

To prepare the filling: Place the pecans on a baking sheet and toast in the oven for 10 minutes, or until lightly browned.

Place the cream in a large bowl and beat with an electric mixer on high speed for 5 minutes, or until stiff peaks form. (When the beaters are lifted out of the cream, they form peaks that remain upright.) Add the confectioners' sugar, cinnamon, cloves, and ginger and mix on low speed for 1 minute, or until combined. Add the pumpkin and mix on low speed until completely incorporated.

To assemble the trifle: Cut the cake into ¾-inch-thick strips. Line the bottom of a trifle bowl or glass bowl with the cake strips, cutting as necessary to make them fit. Sprinkle one quarter of the pecans over the cake and top with one third of the pumpkin mixture. Repeat the layering with the remaining ingredients, forming three layers. (You may only get 2 layers, depending on the size of the bowl you use.) Arrange the remaining one quarter of the pecans on top of the trifle and sprinkle lightly with cinnamon. Refrigerate until ready to serve.

KITCHEN CHEMISTRY

Baking powder contains sodium bicarbonate, but it also includes an acidifying agent (cream of tartar) and a drying agent (usually starch). Baking powder is available as single-acting and double-acting. Single-acting powders are activated by moisture, so recipes containing this type must be baked immediately after mixing. With double-acting powder, some gas is released at room temperature, but the majority is released after the temperature of the dough increases in the oven, so doughs and batters using double-acting baking powder can stand for a while before baking.

GINGERSNAPS WITH PUMPKIN DIP

MAKES ABOUT 6 DOZEN COOKIES AND 1½ CUPS OF DIP

GINGERSNAPS

¾ cup butter

1 cup sugar plus extra for dipping

1 egg

¼ cup molasses

2 teaspoons baking soda

½ teaspoon salt

½ teaspoon ground cinnamon

¼ teaspoon ground cloves

¼ teaspoon ground ginger

2 cups flour

PUMPKIN DIP

4 ounces cream cheese

1 cup confectioners' sugar

1 cup canned pumpkin purée

½ teaspoon ground cinnamon

¼ teaspoon ground ginger

To prepare the gingersnaps: Preheat the oven to 375°F.

Place the butter and sugar in a large bowl and beat with an electric mixer on low speed for 1 minute, or until creamy. Add the egg and molasses and mix on medium speed for 1 minute, or until combined. Add the baking soda, salt, cinnamon, cloves, and ginger and mix for 30 seconds. Add the flour and mix for 2 minutes, or until completely combined. Chill the dough for 30 minutes for easier handling. Place some sugar into a shallow bowl. Roll the dough into ½-inch balls and roll them in the sugar. Place on an ungreased baking sheet about 2 inches apart and bake for 10 minutes, or until set.

To prepare the pumpkin dip: Place the cream cheese in a medium bowl and beat with an electric mixer on medium speed for 2 minutes, or until smooth. Add the confectioners' sugar and mix for 1 minute, or until incorporated. Add the pumpkin, cinnamon, and ginger and mix for 2 minutes, or until completely combined. Refrigerate until ready to serve.

Place the pumpkin dip in a bowl, place it in the center of plate, and arrange the gingersnaps around the bowl.

BIRDS' NESTS

We've made these every Easter for as long as I can remember. A few years ago, I decided that they would make cute place-card holders, so I put the cards in them and placed them around the table. A good thought, but trust me on this one, put a coaster under them or your mom will not be happy when you get chocolate all over her good tablecloth.

M

MAKES ABOUT 10 BIRDS' NESTS

12 ounces chocolate chips

6 ounces butterscotch chips

12 ounces chow mein noodles

Malted milk eggs

Line 10 custard cups or small bowls with plastic wrap.

Place the chocolate and butterscotch chips in a large microwave-safe bowl and microwave on high heat for 90 seconds. Stir the chips. If they are not all melted, place them back in the microwave for 15 seconds at a time, stirring after each time, until they are completely melted. Be careful not to let the mixture start to bubble or it will burn and get gritty. Add the chow mein noodles and stir until completely coated.

Spoon the chow mein noodles into the bowls, pressing the mixture into the bottom and sides to form a $^1/_2$- to $^3/_4$-inch-thick layer. Refrigerate for 10 minutes, or until set. (If the chow mein mixture starts to set before you are finished with all of the bowls, microwave it for 15 seconds, or until it is soft enough to work with.) Pull the plastic away from the bowls to remove the nests. Peel the plastic from the nests and decorate with malted milk eggs. Store at room temperature for up to 1 week.

I love pound cake and am always trying to come up with different ways to serve it. Here I toast the pound cake to warm it up and give it a little more texture, and then layer it with fresh blueberries and strawberries to give it a 4th of July feel. If the red, white, and blue thing is too kitschy for you, it's also really good with peaches and blueberries.

4TH OF JULY POUND CAKE

SERVES 8

1 cup butter plus extra for toasting

1 1/3 cups sugar

1/4 teaspoon salt

1 3/4 cups flour

5 eggs

1 tablespoon milk

2 teaspoons vanilla

1 1/2 cups heavy cream

1/2 cup confectioners' sugar

1 pound (4 cups) fresh strawberries

1 pint (2 cups) fresh blueberries

Preheat the oven to 350°F. Lightly butter or spray a 9 by 5-inch loaf pan.

Place the butter in a large bowl and beat with an electric mixer on medium speed for 2 minutes, or until smooth. Gradually add the sugar and beat for 3 minutes, or until light and fluffy. Add the salt and mix for 10 seconds. Gradually add the flour and mix well. Place the eggs, milk, and vanilla in a separate bowl and whisk until completely combined. Slowly pour the egg mixture into the butter mixture, mixing on low speed until just combined. Pour the batter into the prepared pan and bake for 50 to 60 minutes, or until a toothpick inserted in the center comes out clean. Remove the cake from the pan and cool on a wire rack.

Place the cream in a large bowl and beat with an electric mixer on high speed for 5 minutes, or until soft peaks form. (When the beaters are lifted out of the cream, they form peaks that fold over when the beaters pull away.)

Hull the strawberries and cut them into 1/4-inch-thick slices.

Cut eight 3/4-inch-thick slices from the cooled pound cake. Lightly butter both sides of each piece and place on a griddle pan. Cook over medium heat for 3 to 4 minutes on each side, or until golden brown. Place a

piece of pound cake on each plate and top with the strawberries. Spoon some of the whipped cream over the strawberries and sprinkle with the blueberries.

KITCHEN SHORTCUTS
Use prepared pound cake and omit the pound cake ingredients and preparation.

Use 8 ounces of whipped topping and omit the heavy cream and confectioners' sugar, and the whipped cream preparation.

KITCHEN HISTORY

Pound cakes were first made in northern Europe in the eighteenth century. They were called pound cakes because they contained one pound each of butter, eggs, sugar, and flour. Thankfully, they didn't make them any larger, because "pound-and-a-half cake" just doesn't have the same ring.

This is every little kid's favorite dessert—and one of mine too! It's fun to make with younger siblings or even just after school. You can decorate the top any way you want. We did a cemetery, but you can do it as a garden, or even just a worm hole.

HALLOWEEN DIRT PIE

SERVES 6

CRUST

1 cup chocolate cookie crumbs

¼ cup butter, melted

FILLING

⅔ cup sugar

2 tablespoons cornstarch

Pinch of salt

2 cups milk

1 ounce unsweetened chocolate

2 eggs

1 teaspoon vanilla

TOPPINGS

5 gummy worms

½ cup chocolate cookie crumbs

6 oval sandwich cookies

To prepare the crust: Place the chocolate cookie crumbs in an ungreased 8- or 9-inch pie pan. Add the butter and stir until combined. Press the mixture onto the bottom and sides of the pan with the back of a spoon.

To prepare the filling: Fill a large bowl about halfway with ice cubes and add enough water to almost cover the ice.

Combine the sugar, cornstarch, and salt in a saucepan. Gradually stir in the milk. Add the chocolate and cook over medium heat, stirring constantly, for 5 minutes, or until the mixture comes to a boil. Boil for 1 minute. Beat the eggs slightly in a small bowl. Very slowly whisk some of the hot liquid into the eggs to temper them. Pour the eggs into the pan and cook over low heat, stirring constantly, for 2 minutes, or until the mixture barely begins to bubble. (Do not allow the filling

KITCHEN SHORTCUTS

Use a prepared chocolate cookie crust and omit the crust ingredients and preparation.

Use instant chocolate pudding and omit the filling ingredients and instructions.

to boil or the eggs will curdle.) Remove from the heat and stir in the vanilla.

Strain the filling into a bowl through a fine-mesh sieve and place the bowl in the ice water bath. Stir occasionally for 20 to 30 minutes, or until the filling is cool.

To assemble the pie: Remove the bowl from the ice water bath and gently pour the filling into the crust. Cut the gummy worms in half and insert them around the pie with about 1 inch sticking up. Place the sandwich cookies upright in the filling and sprinkle the cookie crumbs over the top of the pie. Refrigerate for at least 2 hours, or until ready to serve.

When we first found a recipe for bleeding cupcakes, we were very intrigued. Unfortunately, when we tried them we were not impressed. They oozed a little if they were hot, but you can't frost a hot cupcake, so what good is that? So, of course, we had to come up with our own version. They're a little more work, but they definitely bleed.

M

VAMPIRE CUPCAKES

MAKES ABOUT 16 CUPCAKES

CUPCAKES

½ cup butter

1 cup sugar

1 teaspoon vanilla

2 eggs

1 teaspoon baking powder

¼ teaspoon salt

1⅓ cups cake flour

½ cup milk

FILLING

2 ounces cream cheese

¼ cup corn syrup

Red food coloring

To prepare the cupcakes: Preheat the oven to 350°F. Line 16 cupcake cups with paper or foil liners.

Place the butter and sugar in a large bowl and beat with an electric mixer on medium speed for 3 to 4 minutes, or until light and fluffy. Add the vanilla and mix for 30 seconds, or until blended. Add the eggs one at a time, mixing after each addition until completely incorporated. Add the baking powder and salt and mix well. Alternately add the flour and milk, half at a time, mixing well after each addition.

Fill each of the cupcake cups about two-thirds full and bake for 20 to 25 minutes, or until the centers spring back when gently pressed.

To prepare the filling: Place the cream cheese in a bowl and beat with an electric mixer on medium speed for 2 minutes, or until creamy. Add the corn syrup and mix until smooth. Add the food coloring a few drops at a time, mixing after each addition, until the filling is the desired color.

KITCHEN SHORTCUTS
Use yellow or white cake mix and omit the cupcake ingredients and preparation.

FROSTING

½ cup butter

2 cups confectioners' sugar

2 tablespoons milk

1 teaspoon vanilla

Green food coloring

Candy corn

Licorice

Chocolate chips

Cut a 1-inch-wide by 1-inch-deep hole in the center of each cupcake, reserving the cutouts. Spoon a heaping teaspoon of the filling into each cupcake. Remove the bottom half of the cutouts and insert the tops back into the cupcakes.

To prepare the frosting: Place the butter in a bowl and beat with an electric mixer on medium speed for 1 minute, or until creamy. Add the confectioners' sugar, milk, and vanilla and mix on low speed for 1 minute. Add a few drops the food coloring. Increase to medium speed and mix for 2 minutes, or until fluffy.

Spread the frosting over each of the cupcakes and use the candy corn, licorice, and chocolate chips to form vampire faces.

Other Fun Stuff

Funnel cakes are something I get every time I go to a carnival. Since that isn't often enough for my tastes, I figured out how to make them at home, too. Just make sure to open some windows, otherwise your house will smell like a sketchy doughnut shop.

FUNNEL CAKES

MAKES ABOUT 6 FUNNEL CAKES

2 eggs

1 cup milk

1³/₄ cups flour

1 tablespoon sugar

1 teaspoon baking powder

¹/₄ teaspoon salt

Oil for frying

Confectioners' sugar for dusting

Place the eggs in a bowl and whisk until frothy. Whisk in the milk. Add the flour, sugar, baking powder, and salt and whisk until smooth.

Pour 1 inch of oil into a skillet. Heat the oil over medium-high heat for 5 minutes, or until hot. (Test the oil by pouring a small amount of the batter into the pan. The oil should bubble and the batter should cook on one side in about 2 minutes.) Carefully pour the batter into a pitcher. Pour about ¹/₃ cup of the batter into the pan in a tight spiral starting from the center of the pan. Cook for 2 minutes on each side, or until golden brown. Remove from the oil with a fork and place on paper towels to drain. Sprinkle with confectioners' sugar and serve warm. Repeat with remaining batter.

BEIGNETS

We first had these when we went to New Orleans, where they give you about three cups of powdered sugar for each beignet. We learned then that black shirts and beignets do not mix because the powdered sugar gets all over no matter how careful you are. But of course, they are so good that doesn't stop us from eating them. We just change shirts when we're done.

MAKES ABOUT 24 BEIGNETS

1 cup water

⅓ cup butter

¼ teaspoon salt

1 teaspoon vanilla

1 cup flour

1 tablespoon sugar

4 eggs

Oil for frying

Confectioners' sugar for dusting

Place the water, butter, and salt in a saucepan and cook over medium-high heat for 5 minutes, or until it boils. Add the vanilla, then add the flour and sugar all at once. Stir for 1 minute, or until the mixture pulls away from the sides of the pan. Cook, stirring constantly, for 3 more minutes to dry out the dough. Remove from the heat and add the eggs one at a time, beating after each addition until completely incorporated.

Pour about 3 inches of oil into a large saucepan or deep fryer and heat to 375°F. (When a drop of water is added to the oil, it should bubble up immediately.)

Carefully drop 3 or 4 heaping tablespoons of the dough into the hot oil and cook for 10 to 12 minutes, or until golden brown. The beignets should flip over when they are cooked on the first side, if they do not, you will need to flip them over with a slotted spoon. Remove to paper towels to drain. Sprinkle immediately with confectioners' sugar. Repeat with the remaining batter, cooking 3 or 4 beignets at a time. Remove from the oil with a slotted spoon and place on paper towels to drain.

I love these traditional biscuit-type shortcakes because they soak up all of the juice from the fruit. Technically, these should be called fruit shortcakes because you can use almost any kind of fruit. Generally, berries work better, but peaches are good too.

STRAWBERRY SHORTCAKE

SERVES 6

FILLING

1 pound (4 cups) fresh or frozen strawberries

¼ cup sugar

SHORTCAKE

2 cups flour

¼ cup sugar

1 tablespoon baking powder

½ teaspoon salt

⅓ cup cold butter

⅔ cup milk

To prepare the filling: Hull the strawberries and cut them into ¼-inch-thick slices. Place the strawberries in a bowl and stir in the sugar. Refrigerate for 30 minutes, or until the sugar is dissolved.

To prepare the shortcake: Preheat the oven to 400°F.

Place the flour, sugar, baking powder, and salt in a large bowl. Cut the butter into 8 pieces and add to the bowl. Cut the butter into the flour mixture using a pastry cutter or two knives until finely crumbled. Add the milk and stir until the dough just comes together. Place the dough on a lightly floured surface and turn to coat with flour. Fold the dough in half, press down and push forward with the heel of your hand, and turn the dough slightly. Repeat the process 12 times. Roll the dough out to ½ to ¾ inch thick and cut into 4-inch circles with a ring cutter or cookie cutter. Place the shortcakes on an ungreased baking sheet and bake for 12 to 15 minutes, or until they are golden brown.

Kitchen Vocab

The process of folding the dough, pressing, and turning is called **kneading**. Kneading develops the gluten in the flour. But in the case of biscuits including these, it is important not to overknead the dough. It will overdevelop the gluten and make the biscuits tough.

TOPPING

1 cup heavy cream

¼ cup confectioners' sugar

KITCHEN SHORTCUT

Use 8 ounces of whipped topping and omit the topping ingredients and preparation.

To prepare the topping: Place the cream in a large bowl and beat with an electric mixer on medium speed for 2 minutes, or until increased in volume but still very soft. Add the confectioners' sugar and mix for 1 minute, or until combined.

To assemble the shotcakes: Cut each shortcake in half to form 2 circles. Place the bottom halves of the shortcakes on serving plates and top with the strawberries. Place the top of the shortcake over the strawberries and spoon the whipped cream over the shortcake.

The first time my mom made these, my dad's friend Bill was over for dinner. He didn't like the fact that he couldn't get enough of the sauce, so he bunched the edges of the crêpe together and poured the sauce inside. He then dropped the entire thing in his mouth and christened them "crêpe bombs." Needless to say, we kids thought this was a great idea. And so forever more they were crêpe bombs.

CRÊPE BOMBS

SERVES 6

CRÊPES

4 eggs

1 1/3 cups milk

2 tablespoons oil

1 cup flour

1/2 teaspoon salt

To prepare the crêpes: Place the eggs in a blender and pulse a few times to break them up. Add the milk, oil, flour, and salt and blend until smooth.

Heat an 8-inch nonstick sauté pan over medium-high heat. Place a small amount of oil on a paper towel and rub it over the surface of the pan. Pour in 1/4 cup of the crêpe batter and quickly swirl the batter around until it covers the entire bottom of the pan. Cook for 2 minutes, or until the crêpe is set in the center. Loosen the edges with a rubber spatula and turn the crêpe over. Cook for 1 minute and remove from the pan. Repeat the process with the remaining batter, oiling the pan before cooking each crêpe. The cooked crêpes can be stacked on top of each other and gently pulled apart

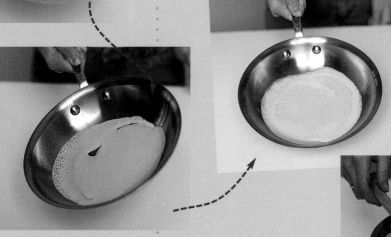

SAUCE

½ cup butter

½ cup firmly packed brown sugar

1 tablespoon grated orange peel

½ cup orange juice

when you are ready to use them, or they can be separated by pieces of waxed paper for easier handling.

To prepare the sauce: Place the butter in a small saucepan and cook over medium-high heat for 2 minutes, or until the butter is melted. Add the brown sugar, orange peel, and orange juice and bring to a boil. Serve immediately or reheat before serving.

Fold the crêpes in quarters, arrange 2 on each plate, and spoon the sauce over the crêpes. (Or you can eat them as bombs, the way we do.)

Warm apples, pastry, and caramel. Need I say more? This is really quick and easy to make. Just serve it with a little vanilla ice cream and it is super excellent.

APPLE DUMPLINGS WITH CARAMEL SAUCE

SERVES 4

DUMPLINGS

4 apples

¹/₂ cup firmly packed brown sugar

¹/₂ teaspoon ground cinnamon

1 sheet puff pastry dough

1 egg

CARAMEL SAUCE

¹/₂ cup sugar

¹/₄ cup water

¹/₂ cup heavy cream

2 tablespoons butter

KITCHEN SHORTCUT

Warm ³/₄ cup of prepared caramel sauce in the microwave and omit the caramel sauce ingredients and preparation.

To prepare the dumplings: Preheat the oven to 400°F.

Peel and core the apples, keeping them in one piece.

Place the brown sugar and cinnamon in a small bowl and stir until combined.

Cut the puff pastry sheet into 4 squares. Place an apple in the center of each square and pack the core with the brown sugar mixture. Pull up all four corners of the pastry, wet the points slightly, and press together to seal them. Lightly beat the egg and brush it on the pastry. Place the apples in an ungreased baking pan and bake for 30 minutes, or until the pastry is golden brown.

To prepare the caramel sauce: Place the sugar in a small saucepan and pour in the water, making sure all of the sugar gets wet. Cook over medium-high heat, without stirring, for 10 minutes, or until the sugar turns golden brown. Add the cream and butter and stir until smooth. (The sugar may harden when you add the cream, but continue cooking and it will melt again.)

Spoon some of the caramel sauce in the center of each plate and top with a warm apple dumpling.

> I love peppermint ice cream, but since they only sell it during the holidays, I had to learn to make it myself. Making it into sandwiches not only adds a little bit of chocolate, it makes it portable, too. What could be better than that?

M

PEPPERMINT ICE CREAM SANDWICHES

SERVES 12

ICE CREAM

3 cups half-and-half

6 egg yolks

¾ cup sugar

¾ cup crushed peppermint candies (about 30)

BROWNIES

3 ounces unsweetened chocolate

¾ cup butter

1½ cups sugar

3 eggs

1½ teaspoons vanilla

¾ cup flour

¾ teaspoon baking powder

To prepare the ice cream: Fill a large bowl about halfway with ice cubes and add enough water to almost cover the ice.

Place the half-and-half in a large saucepan and cook over medium-high heat for 5 minutes, or until it comes to a boil. Whisk together the egg yolks and sugar in a bowl and slowly whisk in some of the hot half-and-half to temper the eggs. Pour the eggs into the pan, add about half of the peppermint candies, and cook over medium-low heat for 2 to 3 minutes, or until the mixture coats the back of a metal spoon. (Do not allow the mixture to boil or the eggs will curdle.)

Strain the mixture into a bowl through a fine-mesh sieve and place the bowl in the ice water bath. Stir occasionally for 20 to 30 minutes, or until the mixture is cool. Remove the bowl from the ice water bath and refrigerate for 1 hour, or until completely chilled. Freeze in an ice cream maker according to the manufacturer's directions. When the ice cream is frozen, add the remaining peppermint candies and spin for 1 minute to distribute them. Place the ice cream in an airtight container and freeze until ready to use.

To prepare the brownies: Preheat the oven to 350°F. Line an 11 by 17-inch baking sheet with parchment paper and lightly butter or spray the parchment paper and the sides of the pan.

Place the chocolate in a large microwave-safe bowl and microwave on high heat for 1 minute, then stir. If the chocolate is not all melted, place it back in the microwave for 15 seconds at a time, stirring after each time, until it is completely melted. Be careful not to let the chocolate start to bubble or it will burn and get gritty. Add the butter and stir until it is melted. Add the sugar, eggs, and vanilla and stir until completely incorporated. Add the flour and baking powder and stir until just combined. Spread the batter in the prepared pan and bake for 18 minutes, or until set in the center. Remove from the oven and cool completely.

To assemble the ice cream sandwiches: Flip the entire sheet of brownies onto a cutting board and cut the rectangle in half crosswise. Place 1 half on a piece of plastic wrap large enough to wrap the entire piece with a few inches to spare. Spread a $\frac{1}{2}$-inch layer of the peppermint ice cream on the brownie and top with the remaining brownie half. Wrap tightly in the plastic wrap and freeze for at least 1 hour, or until ready to serve. Remove the plastic wrap and cut into 12 ice cream sandwiches. (The ice cream sandwiches can be wrapped individually and frozen for up to 1 week.)

I came up with this idea while working the graveyard shift at a restaurant. There was always a lull between three and six o'clock, leaving the cooks and me to invent our own variations using the ingredients in the restaurant. We've worked on the recipe since then, and now these sweet little chimichangas are really tasty.

M

PEACH-CHEESECAKE CHIMICHANGAS

SERVES 8

4 ounces cream cheese

$1/3$ cup sweetened
condensed milk

1 tablespoon lemon juice

$1/2$ teaspoon vanilla

2 peaches

8 6-inch flour tortillas

Oil for frying

Confectioners' sugar for
dusting

Place the cream cheese in a large bowl and beat with an electric mixer on medium speed for 2 minutes, or until creamy. Add the sweetened condensed milk and mix for 1 minute, or until smooth. Stir in the lemon juice and vanilla and refrigerate until ready to use.

Peel the peaches and cut each one into 16 wedges.

Place a tortilla on a flat surface and spoon about $1/4$ cup of the cream cheese mixture in a 1 by 3-inch rectangle near the bottom edge of the tortilla. Lay 4 peach slices over the cream cheese. Fold in both sides of the tortilla then roll it up forming a 3-inch long chimichanga. Seal the chimichanga by threading a toothpick or small skewer

kitchen safety

Make sure to use a pot at least 3 inches deeper than the oil when you are deep-frying. This allows room for the oil to bubble up without running over the sides of the pan. In the unlikely event that you do have a grease fire, remember to pour baking soda on it to put it out. Never use water on a grease fire. It just makes it splatter and spread. Not good.

through the tortilla. Repeat with the remaining ingredients to make 8 chimichangas.

Pour about 2 inches of oil into a large saucepan or deep fryer. Heat the oil to 375°F. (When a drop of water is added to the oil, it should bubble up immediately.) Carefully place a few of the chimichangas into the oil and cook for 2 to 3 minutes on each side, or until golden brown. Remove to paper towels to drain. Repeat with the remaining chimichangas. Remove the toothpicks, sprinkle the chimichangas with confectioners' sugar, and serve warm.

M

My great-grandmother always served these traditional German meringue tortes with berries and ice cream. A few years ago when we were trying to make fat-free desserts, we tried them with sorbet instead. They were so good that now we eat them that way all the time. They are super simple to make, so when I'm feeling creative I put the uncooked meringue into a pastry bag and make different shapes or letters.

SCHAUM TORTES WITH RASPBERRY SORBET

SERVES 10

SORBET

1 cup sugar

1 cup water

1½ pints (3 cups) fresh or
  frozen raspberries

SCHAUM TORTES

4 egg whites

½ teaspoon cream of tartar

1 cup sugar

1 teaspoon vanilla

To prepare the sorbet: Place the sugar and water in a small saucepan and cook over medium-high heat, stirring occasionally, for 5 minutes, or until the mixture comes to a boil. Boil for 1 minute, remove from the heat, and let cool to room temperature.

Place the raspberries and the cooled sugar mixture in a blender and blend for 30 seconds, or until smooth. Strain through a fine-mesh sieve. (Stirring the purée in the sieve will help push it through.) Refrigerate until very cold. Freeze in an ice cream maker according to the manufacturer's directions. Place in an airtight container and freeze for at least 2 hours before serving.

To prepare the tortes: Preheat the oven to 250°F.

Place the egg whites and cream of tartar in a large bowl and beat with an electric mixer on high speed for 2 minutes, or until soft peaks form. (When the beaters are lifted out of the cream, they form peaks that fold over when the beaters pull away.) Add the sugar and vanilla and beat for 1 minute, or until thick and glossy. Place a brown paper bag on a baking sheet. Drop a heaping tablespoon of the meringue onto the bag, spread into a 3-inch circle, and form a well in the center. Repeat with the remaining meringue to make 10 tortes.

Kitchen Vocab

The mixture of sugar and water that's made for the sorbet is called **simple syrup**. It's a frequently used item in a pastry kitchen. It can be flavored and brushed on cakes, used for poaching fruit, or, as in this case, used for making sorbet.

Bake for 1 hour, then turn off the oven and prop the oven door slightly open by placing a wooden spoon in the opening. Leave the tortes in the oven for 1 hour, or until completely cool. (Schaum tortes may be kept in an airtight container for several days.)

Place a torte on each plate and top with a scoop of sorbet.

✱ Kitchen Tip ✱

Making sorbet is simple, but because every fruit has a different sugar content, getting the sweetness right can be trying. Here is a trick my mom learned from a chef friend that makes it come out perfectly every time: After you mix the fruit and simple syrup, place a raw egg (in the shell) in the mixture. If the egg floats with only about a quarter-sized part of the egg raised out of the mixture, you have the perfect balance. If the egg floats too high, you need to add more water. If the egg sinks, you need to add more simple syrup. Works every time.

M

This is my family's standard movie-night treat. When I was younger, I was the designated caramel corn maker. It's really easy 'cause you can do everything in the microwave. Just make sure you shake up the bag enough so all the popcorn gets coated. And be careful when you pour it onto the baking sheet; it's really hot and sticky.

MICROWAVE CARAMEL CORN

MAKES 4 QUARTS

2 bags microwave popcorn

1 cup firmly packed brown sugar

1/2 cup butter

1/4 cup corn syrup

1/2 teaspoon salt

1/2 teaspoon baking soda

Spray the inside of a microwave-proof cooking bag or a brown paper grocery bag with vegetable cooking spray.

Pop the microwave popcorn according to the directions.

Place the brown sugar, butter, corn syrup, and salt in a 2-quart microwave-safe bowl and microwave on high heat for 4 to 5 minutes, or until it boils. Add the baking soda and stir until foamy.

Pour the popcorn into the prepared bag and pour the sugar mixture over the popcorn. Microwave on high heat for 1 minute, remove from the microwave, and shake well. Cook for 45 seconds and shake well. Cook for 30 seconds and shake well. Cook for 15 seconds and shake well. Pour out onto a baking sheet and let cool.

✳ Kitchen Tip ✳

We use a silicone baking mat whenever we are working with something sticky like caramel corn or something very delicate like a tuile. These mats are the ultimate nonstick surface. You can pick up the silicone baking mat and peel off the tuiles without breaking any. Our mom got one years ago from a restaurant supply place. But now they are available everywhere. They cost around $15, but if you take care of them, they last forever.

AFTER DINNER MINTS

I thought it would be really cool to make my own after dinner mints. After botching four batches I thought better of that idea and decided to make taffy instead. When I was cutting the taffy into pieces, I dropped them into confectioners' sugar the way the mint recipe said to. Imagine my surprise when I tried some the next day and discovered the after dinner mints that I had been trying to make all along. Another successful mistake.

MAKES ABOUT 100 PIECES

1 1/2 cups sugar

1/4 cup water

1/2 cup corn syrup

2 tablespoons butter

Pinch of salt

1/2 teaspoon peppermint flavoring

Food coloring (optional)

1 pound confectioners' sugar

Cornstarch

Kitchen Tip

When you are adding flavoring to a boiling liquid, always wait until it has cooled at least enough to stop bubbling. If you add the flavoring too soon, it will boil off and leave a bitter flavor or no flavor at all.

Lightly butter or spray a baking sheet.

Place the sugar, water, corn syrup, butter, and salt in a large saucepan and cook over medium-high heat, stirring occasionally, for 10 minutes, or until it reaches 270°F. (When a small amount is dropped in ice water, it will form threads that will bend.) Remove from the heat and let stand until it completely stops bubbling.

Pour the mixture onto the prepared baking sheet and let stand for 5 minutes, or until cool enough to handle. Drizzle the peppermint flavoring and food coloring over the candy. Dip your fingers in a little cornstarch and pull the candy straight out without twisting. Fold the candy over and continue pulling and folding until it is lukewarm and creamy looking. Stretch the candy into a 1/2-inch rope. Pour the confectioners' sugar into a baking pan. Cut the candy into 1/2-inch pieces, toss the sugar to coat, and let it stand overnight.

Making lollipops is really fun. You can make them any flavor or color that you choose. Sometimes we stay on the straight and narrow and make the colors correspond to the flavors, and other times we don't. It's kind of fun to see someone's face when they pick up a purple lollipop expecting it to be grape and it's really lemon.

CINNAMON LOLLIPOPS

MAKES ABOUT 25 LOLLIPOPS

1 cup sugar

1/3 cup corn syrup

1/2 cup water

1/4 teaspoon cream of tartar

1/2 teaspoon cinnamon flavoring

Red food coloring

Lollipop sticks

Place a baking sheet upside down on a flat surface and generously oil or spray the pan and a 2-cup heat-proof measuring cup with a pour spout.

Place the sugar, corn syrup, water, and cream of tartar in a large saucepan and cook over medium-high heat, stirring constantly with a wooden spoon, for 5 minutes, or until the sugar is dissolved. Continue to stir for 5 minutes, or until it begins to boil, occasionally brushing the sides of the pan with a pastry brush dipped in warm water. (This dissolves any sugar crystals on the sides of the pan.) Stop stirring as soon as it begins to boil.

KITCHEN CHEMISTRY

Adding corn syrup to sugar will help keep it from crystallizing. Corn syrup contains long chains of glucose molecules, which act as an interfering agent to keep the melted sucrose molecules (sugar) from forming crystals again.

Place a candy thermometer in the pan, being careful not to let it touch the bottom or sides of the pan. (The pan is hotter than the contents and will give you a false reading.) Allow the syrup to boil for 10 minutes, or until it reaches 300°F. (To test for the hard-crack stage, drop a little of the sugar into ice water. It should separate into threads that are hard and brittle.) Immediately remove the pan from the heat and let the syrup cool to 275°F, or until completely stops bubbling. Add the cinnamon flavoring and food coloring and stir quickly. Pour the syrup

into the prepared measuring cup and quickly pour 2-inch rounds on the parchment paper. Place a lollipop stick at least one quarter of the way into each sucker and twist to ensure the stick adheres. (Skewers cut in half also work well as sticks.)

Let the lollipops cool for 15 minutes, or until they are hard. Wrap each one in plastic wrap and seal with tape or ribbon.

This is a really fancy looking dessert that is actually quite easy to make. The most difficult part is working with the phyllo dough. Just make sure to keep it under a barely damp towel so it doesn't dry out and try to work as fast as you can. Don't get frustrated; if a few sheets tear or get stuck together, just throw them out. There are plenty in each box.

CHERRY-ALMOND SWIRL

SERVES 6

2 (15-ounce) cans black or sweet cherries

2 tablespoons sugar

1 tablespoon cornstarch

¾ teaspoon almond extract

1 egg

21 sheets phyllo dough

½ cup butter, melted

½ cup ground almonds

Confectioners' sugar for dusting

Drain the cherries, reserving ¾ cup of the juice. Place the cherry juice in a small saucepan. Add the sugar and cornstarch and cook over medium-high heat, stirring constantly, for 2 to 3 minutes, or until it comes to a boil. Remove the pan from the heat and stir in the cherries and almond extract.

Preheat the oven to 375°F. Place the egg in a small bowl and beat well.

Unroll the phyllo dough and cover with damp paper towels. (Make sure you cover the phyllo every time you take a sheet or it will dry out.) Lay one sheet of phyllo

on a flat surface and brush the entire surface with some of the melted butter. Sprinkle some of the almonds and confectioners' sugar over the butter and top with another phyllo sheet. Brush the phyllo sheet with the butter, sprinkle with almonds and confectioners' sugar, and cover with another phyllo sheet. Starting at one end of the long edge of the phyllo, spread about $^{1}/_{3}$ cup of the cherries along the bottom edge, stopping about 1 inch from the end. Loosely roll the phyllo into a long cigar shape. Set it seam side down and brush one side of the roll with the egg. (If you roll it too tightly, the phyllo will crack when you form the spiral.) Starting in the center of an ungreased 9-inch round cake pan, form a spiral with the egg side toward the center.

Repeat the process with the remaining phyllo sheets and filling, brushing the ends with egg and overlapping them about 1 inch each time to form a continuous spiral. Brush the top of the spiral with butter and bake for 40 to 45 minutes, or until the phyllo is golden brown. Cool for 15 minutes and serve warm.

TUXEDOED STRAWBERRIES

The first time I saw these, I thought they were the cutest things I'd ever seen and didn't want to eat them. After they dried out in the refrigerator, I realized that it didn't make much sense to waste them. I still think it's kind of sad to eat them because they look so cool, but not sad enough to stop me from eating them.

MAKES 12 STRAWBERRIES

2 ounces white chocolate

12 skewers

12 large fresh strawberries

1 cup chocolate chips

1 tablespoon butter

Place the white chocolate in a microwave-safe bowl and microwave on high heat for 1 minute, then stir. If the chocolate is not all melted, place it back in the microwave for 15 seconds at a time, stirring after each time, until it is completely melted.

Place a skewer partway into the top of each strawberry. Dip one side of each strawberry into the white chocolate, leaving a scant $\frac{1}{2}$ inch at the top uncovered. Place the skewers into a canister full of sugar to hold them upright. Let stand for 5 minutes, or until the white chocolate is set.

Place the chocolate chips in a microwave-safe bowl and microwave on high heat for 1 minute, then stir. If the chocolate is not all melted, place it back in the microwave for 15 seconds at a time, stirring after each time, until it is completely melted. Be careful not to let the chocolate start to bubble or it will burn and get gritty. Add the butter and stir until smooth.

Dip each side of the strawberries in the chocolate, covering the entire strawberry except a $\frac{3}{4}$-inch triangle of the white chocolate. Place the skewers back in the canister of sugar. Dip a toothpick or skewer in the chocolate and place 2 dots on the white chocolate to simulate buttons. Let stand for 15 minutes, or until set, then refrigerate until ready to serve

M

Whether you roll caramel apples in chopped peanuts or leave them plain, they are delicious and really easy to make. I also like to cover them in chopped up leftover Halloween candy.

CARAMEL APPLES

MAKES 8 CARAMEL APPLES

2½ cups heavy cream

2½ cups sugar

¾ cup corn syrup

¼ teaspoon cream of tartar

½ cup butter

1 teaspoon vanilla

8 craft sticks or skewers

8 large, cold apples

½ cup chopped peanuts

Place the cream, sugar, corn syrup, and cream of tartar in a saucepan and cook over medium-high heat, stirring occasionally for 15 minutes, or until it reaches 246°F. (Don't panic if the caramel seems too light. It should be a pale yellow color, much lighter than store-bought caramel.) Remove the pan from the heat and stir in the butter and vanilla. Pour the caramel into a heatproof bowl. Let the caramel cool for about 20 minutes, or until it reaches 200°F.

Insert a craft stick in the stem end of each apple. Dip an apple into the caramel, coating all but the very top of the apple. Lift the apple out of the caramel and hold it over the bowl for a few seconds to allow the excess caramel to drip off. Turn the apple caramel side up and hold for several seconds to set the caramel. Roll the bottom and sides of the apple in the peanuts and set on a foil-lined tray to cool. Repeat with the remaining apples.

✳ Kitchen Tip ✳

Making candy or caramels is easy . . . if your thermometer is correct. We know that sounds pretty basic, but we have ruined countless batches because our thermometer was off. We recently stumbled across an easy fix: place your thermometer in a pot of boiling water without letting it touch the bottom or sides and look at what the temperature reads. Water boils at 212°F. If your thermometer reads 200°F, then you know you have to cook to 12° higher than the recipe states. If your thermometer reads 220°F, then you cook to 8° less.

DRIED FRUIT ROLLS

Here is a really healthy sweet snack. Just think, not only are there no preservatives, but you can pronounce every ingredient in it. Plus you have the bragging rights—you actually made them yourself. I think that's pretty impressive. We have made these with apples and strawberries, but almost any type of fruit would work well.

MAKES 12 ROLLS

4 cups peeled and chopped apples (about 6)

Pinch of salt

Pinch of ground cinnamon

1/2 cup honey

1 tablespoon lemon juice

❋ ❋ Kitchen Tip

You will notice that in the directions we tell you to cover the blender with a towel and hold the top down. That may seem like overkill, but it's not. When hot liquids are blended, they cause the air in the blender to expand. It can blow the top right off the blender and spray hot ingredients all over you and all over the kitchen. Trust us on this one. We learned the hard way.

Preheat the oven to 175°F. Line an 11 by 17-inch baking sheet with waxed paper and thoroughly butter or spray the paper.

Place the apples in a saucepan. Add enough water to just cover the apples and cook over medium-high heat for 15 minutes, or until very soft. Drain the apples and place them in a blender. Add the salt, cinnamon, honey, and lemon juice. Place a towel over the blender lid and, holding the lid on, blend for 30 seconds, or until completely smooth.

Spread the purée in the prepared pan in an even layer about 1/8 to 1/4 inch thick. Place in the oven for 3 hours, or until dry. Remove the fruit from the pan and peel off the waxed paper. Cut into 12 pieces, roll in waxed paper to keep the fruit from sticking together, and store in an airtight container until ready to serve.

KITCHEN HISTORY

Fruit leathers have been around for many centuries. They were developed as a way to preserve fruits so they could be enjoyed many months past their season. There is actually documentation that Lewis and Clark snacked on fruit leather during their famous expedition.

Fancy Stuff

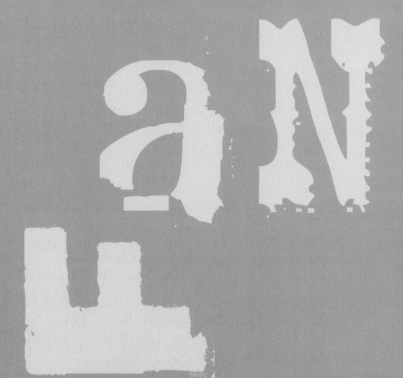

This is a great dessert to serve if you want to make an impression. We always used to buy phyllo dough in 11 by 17-inch sheets, but lately we have only been able to get 9 by 14-inch sheets. It doesn't matter what size you use, except if you buy the smaller sheets, you will use 9 sheets, repeat the assembly process an extra time, and serve 3 instead of 2 per serving.

WHITE CHOCOLATE-CHERRY PHYLLO TRIANGLES WITH CHERRY SAUCE

SERVES 6

TRIANGLES

1 cup dried cherries

$^1/_2$ cup sugar

$^1/_2$ cup water

3 ounces white chocolate

6 sheets phyllo dough

$^1/_2$ cup butter, melted

Confectioner's sugar for dusting

SAUCE

1 cup dried cherries

$^1/_2$ cup orange juice

$^1/_2$ cup water

1 cup sugar

To prepare the triangles: Place the dried cherries, sugar, and water in a small saucepan. Cook over medium-high heat for 20 minutes, or until most of the liquid is absorbed.

Chop the white chocolate into small pieces.

Preheat the oven to 375°F.

Unroll the phyllo dough and cover with damp paper towels. (Make sure you cover the phyllo every time you take a sheet or it will dry out.) Lay one sheet of phyllo on a flat surface and brush the entire surface with some of the butter. Sprinkle some confectioners' sugar over the butter and top with another phyllo sheet. Brush the phyllo with butter and sprinkle with confectioners' sugar. Top with another sheet of phyllo and cut the sheets into 6 strips.

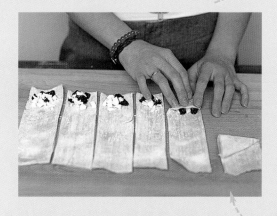

Spoon about 1 tablespoon of the cherries on the end of each strip and top with some of the white chocolate. Pull up the corner of one phyllo strip to form a triangle. Fold the triangle up and over in a tight flag fold until you reach the end of the strip, being careful to keep the corners tight. Brush the end of the phyllo with butter and press to seal. Place the triangle on an ungreased baking sheet and repeat the process with the remaining strips. When all 6 strips are complete, repeat the entire process with the remaining phyllo and filling. Brush the tops of the triangles with butter and bake for 15 minutes, or until golden brown.

To prepare the sauce: Place the cherries, orange juice, water, and sugar in a small saucepan and cook over medium-low heat for 20 minutes, or until the liquid is reduced by half.

Place 2 of the triangles on each plate and top with some of the sauce.

Cooks in New England historically have been known for their cakes and pies, and there seems to be a very thin dividing line between the two. This was probably called a pie because it was made in pie pans, which were more prevalent than cake pans. So, is it a cake or a pie? I say, it tastes really good so who cares what they call it.

INDIVIDUAL BOSTON CREAM PIES

SERVES 6

FILLING

¹/₄ cup sugar

1¹/₂ tablespoons cornstarch

Pinch of salt

1 cup milk

2 egg yolks

¹/₂ teaspoon vanilla

1 teaspoon butter

CAKE

¹/₂ cup butter

1 cup sugar

1 teaspoon vanilla

2 eggs

1 teaspoon baking powder

Pinch of salt

1¹/₃ cups cake flour

¹/₂ cup milk

FROSTING

¹/₂ cup chocolate chips

¹/₂ cup heavy cream

¹/₄ cup confectioners' sugar

To prepare the filling: Fill a large bowl about halfway with ice cubes and add enough water to almost cover the ice.

Combine the sugar, cornstarch, and salt in a saucepan. Gradually add the milk. Cook over medium heat, stirring frequently, for 5 minutes, or until the mixture comes to a boil. Boil for 1 minute. Beat the egg yolks slightly in a small bowl. Very slowly whisk some of the hot liquid into the eggs to temper them. Pour the eggs into the pan and cook over low heat, stirring constantly, for 2 minutes, or until the mixture barely begins to bubble. (Do not allow the filling to boil or the eggs will curdle.) Remove from the heat and stir in the vanilla and butter.

Strain the filling into a bowl through a fine-mesh sieve and place the bowl in the ice water bath. Stir occasionally for 20 to 30 minutes, or until the filling is cool. Remove the bowl from the ice water bath, lay a piece of plastic wrap directly on the filling, and refrigerate for 1 hour, or until completely chilled.

To prepare the cake: Preheat the oven to 350°F. Lightly butter or spray an 11 by 15-inch baking sheet.

Place the butter and sugar in a large bowl and beat with an electric mixer on medium speed for 3 to 4 minutes, or until light and fluffy. Add the vanilla extract and mix for 30 seconds, or until blended. Add the eggs one at a time, mixing after each addition until completely incorporated. Add the baking powder and salt and mix well. Alternately add the flour and milk one third at a time, mixing well after each addition. Pour the batter into the prepared pan and bake for 25 to 30 minutes, or until the cake springs back when gently pressed in the center. Remove from the oven and cool in the pan.

To prepare the frosting: Place the chocolate in a microwave-safe bowl and microwave on high heat for 1 minute, then stir. If the chocolate is not all melted, place it back in the microwave for 15 seconds at a time, stirring after each time, until it is completely melted. Be careful not to let the chocolate start to bubble or it will burn and get gritty. Add the cream and confectioners' sugar and stir until smooth.

To assemble the pies: Cut 12 circles from the cake using a 3-inch ring cutter or cookie cutter. Place one of the cake circles on each plate and top with some of the filling. Place another cake circle on the pudding and pour some of the frosting on top of each cake.

This variation on cheesecake is really super cute. We just cut 12 pieces out of the pan, but you could easily cut them into smaller 1 by 2-inch pieces and serve them on a dessert tray. How cute would that be?

WHITE CHOCOLATE-COVERED CHEESECAKE DOMINOS

SERVES 12

CRUST

1½ cups graham cracker crumbs

¼ cup butter, melted

¼ cup sugar

FILLING

32 ounces cream cheese

1¼ cups sugar

4 eggs

2 teaspoons vanilla

¼ cup heavy cream

¼ cup sour cream

TOPPING

24 ounces white chocolate

¼ cup chocolate chips

Preheat the oven to 325°F.

To prepare the crust: Place the crust ingredients in an ungreased 9 by 13-inch pan and stir until combined. Firmly press the mixture into the bottom of the pan and refrigerate until ready to use.

To prepare the filling: Place the cream cheese in a large bowl and beat with an electric mixer on medium speed for 2 minutes, or until completely smooth. Add the sugar and beat, scraping the sides of the bowl occasionally, for 2 minutes, or until combined. Add the eggs and vanilla and mix for 2 to 3 minutes, or until smooth. Add the heavy cream and sour cream and stir with a spoon until just incorporated.

Gently pour the filling over the crust and place the cheesecake pan in a larger baking pan. Place the pans in the oven and pour enough hot water into the larger baking pan to come halfway up the sides of the cheesecake pan. Bake for 1 hour. Turn off the oven and prop the oven door open slightly by placing a wooden spoon in the opening. Leave the cheesecake in the oven for 1 hour, or until the oven is completely cool.

To prepare the topping: Place the white chocolate in a microwave-safe bowl and microwave on high heat for 1 minute, then stir. If the chocolate is not all melted,

place it back in the microwave for 15 seconds at a time, stirring after each time, until it is completely melted. Place the white chocolate into a measuring cup with a pour spout.

Cut the cooled cheesecake in half lengthwise, then cut each half into 6 even pieces, forming 12 pieces that are approximately 2 by 4$^1/_2$ inches. Set a wire cooling rack atop parchment or waxed paper and transfer the cheesecake pieces to the rack, spacing them about 1 inch apart. Pour the white chocolate over the cheesecakes, starting at one end and pouring in a smooth back-and-forth motion to cover each piece entirely in a smooth layer. (If necessary, you can smooth the chocolate with a spatula while it is still hot.) Line a baking sheet with parchment or waxed paper, transfer the cheesecakes to the prepared pan, and refrigerate for 10 minutes, or until the chocolate is set.

Place the chocolate chips in a microwave-safe bowl and microwave on high heat for 1 minute, then stir. If the chocolate is not all melted, place it back in the microwave for 15 seconds at a time, stirring after each time, until it is completely melted.

Dip the flat end of a skewer into the melted chocolate chips and make te dots on the tops of the cheesecakes to resemble the dominos. Place the remaining chocolate on a plate or piece of waxed paper. Dip the flat end of a knife into the chocolate and form a line across the middle of each domino. Refrigerate until ready to serve.

KITCHEN HISTORY

Although we didn't come up with anything noteworthy in our research on cheesecake, we did find a related tidbit we had to share. Granted, it's loosely related, but it does have to do with cheese. The curds and whey that Miss Muffet was munching on before her uninvited guest arrived were actually the sixteenth-century precursor to cottage cheese: soured milk curds with the liquid that leaches off. Yum.

Everyone loves banana splits. Well, when I say everyone, I really mean me. This is a pretty traditional banana split except we serve it in a banana tuile instead of a dish and we use caramel instead of pineapple. Who puts pineapple on ice cream anyway? Making all of the ice creams is time-consuming, so you can use store-bought, but you will miss out on the best strawberry ice cream ever.

BANANA SPLITS IN BANANA TUILE CUPS

SERVES 4

ICE CREAMS

12 ounces (3 cups) fresh or frozen strawberries

¼ cup honey

½ cup chocolate chips

1 vanilla bean or 2 teaspoons vanilla

4½ cups half-and-half

9 egg yolks

1 cup sugar

To prepare the ice creams: Hull and slice the strawberries and place them in a saucepan with the honey. Cook over medium-high heat for 10 minutes, or until the strawberries are soft. Remove from the heat and let cool.

Fill 1 medium and 1 large bowl about halfway with ice cubes and add enough water to almost cover the ice.

Place the chocolate chips in a medium bowl.

Cut the vanilla bean in half lengthwise and scrape out the seeds. Place the seeds and pod in a large saucepan with the half-and-half and cook over medium-high heat for 5 minutes, or until it comes to a boil. Remove from the heat and let steep for 10 minutes. (If you are using vanilla extract, omit the steeping and add the vanilla after straining.) Place the pan back on the heat and bring to a boil. Whisk together the egg yolks and sugar in a bowl and slowly whisk in some of the hot half-and-half to temper the eggs. Pour the egg mixture into the pan and cook over low heat, stirring constantly, for 1 minute, or until the mixture coats the back of a metal spoon. Strain through a fine-mesh sieve and pour one third of the mixture into the bowl with the chocolate and

[continued]

the remaining two thirds into a large bowl. Stir the chocolate ice cream until all of the chips are melted, then place both bowls in the ice water baths. Stir occasionally for 20 to 30 minutes, or until cool.

Divide the larger bowl of ice cream into 2 bowls. Stir two thirds of the strawberry mixture into one of the bowls, reserving the remainder to use as strawberry sauce. Refrigerate all 3 bowls for 1 hour, or until completely chilled. Freeze separately in an ice cream maker according to the manufacturer's directions. Place the ice creams in airtight containers and freeze until ready to use.

To prepare the tuiles: Preheat the oven to 300°F. Butter or spray 2 baking sheets.

Place the banana in a bowl and mash with a fork. Add the flour and sugar and stir until smooth. Thinly spread the batter into four 7- to 8-inch circles on the prepared baking sheets. Bake for 15 minutes, or until just set in the middle. Quickly remove the tuiles from the pan and drape them over small inverted bowls to cool. (Only remove 1 pan from the oven at a time because the tuiles cool quickly and will become too crisp to form into cups.)

To prepare the hot fudge sauce: Place the sugar, brown sugar, cocoa, flour, and salt in saucepan. Add the evaporated milk and butter and cook over medium heat, stirring frequently, for 8 minutes, or until it comes to a boil. Boil, stirring constantly, for 5 minutes, then remove from the heat and stir in the vanilla. (Extra sauce can be refrigerated in an airtight container for up to 1 month and reheated in the microwave.)

To prepare the caramel sauce: Place the sugar in a small sauté pan and pour in the water, making sure all

KITCHEN HISTORY

The first banana split was made in 1904 at Strickler's Drug Store in Pennsylvania. It consisted of one split banana, two or three scoops of ice cream, and chocolate and strawberry sauces. Which just goes to prove our point. Pineapple sauce does not belong on ice cream.

of the sugar gets wet. Cook over medium-high heat, without stirring, for 10 minutes, or until the sugar turns golden brown. Add the cream and butter to the pan and stir until smooth. (The sugar may harden when you add the cream, but continue cooking and it will melt again.) Remove from the heat and let cool.

To assemble the banana splits: Place each tuile cup in a shallow bowl. Place a scoop of vanilla, strawberry, and chocolate ice cream in each cup. Cut the bananas diagonally into $1/4$- to $3/8$-inch-thick slices and place them alongside the ice cream in each bowl. Spoon some of the caramel sauce over the vanilla ice cream, the reserved strawberry sauce over the strawberry ice cream, and the hot fudge sauce over the chocolate ice cream. Serve immediately.

We call this a "company dessert." We only make it when we have company coming over. It's time-consuming to put together, but it's guaranteed to impress your guests. None of the steps are difficult; there are just a lot of them. The good news is this is best made a day ahead, so all the work can be done long before your guests arrive.

WHITE CHOCOLATE MOUSSE CAKE WITH RASPBERRIES

SERVES 12

CAKE

¹/₂ cup butter

1 cup sugar

1 teaspoon vanilla

2 eggs

1 teaspoon baking powder

¹/₄ teaspoon salt

1¹/₃ cups cake flour

¹/₂ cup milk

MOUSSE

1 cup milk

3 egg yolks

¹/₃ cup sugar

2 tablespoons cornstarch

1 teaspoon vanilla

9 ounces white chocolate

1¹/₂ cups heavy cream

2 pints (4 cups) fresh raspberries

To prepare the cake: Preheat the oven to 350°F. Lightly butter or spray a 9-inch cake pan.

Place the butter and sugar in a large bowl and beat with an electric mixer on medium speed, occasionally scraping the sides of the bowl, for 3 to 4 minutes, or until light and fluffy. Add the vanilla and mix for 30 seconds, or until blended. Add the eggs one at a time, mixing after each addition until completely incorporated. Add the baking powder and salt and mix well. Alternately add the flour and milk one third at a time, mixing well after each addition. Pour the batter into the prepared pan and bake for 35 to 40 minutes, or until the cake springs back when gently pressed in the center. Remove the cake from the pan and cool on a wire rack.

To prepare the mousse: Fill a large bowl about halfway with ice cubes and add enough water to almost cover the ice.

Place the milk in a large saucepan and cook over medium-high heat for 5 minutes, or until it begins to boil. Whisk together the egg yolks, sugar, and cornstarch in a bowl and very slowly whisk some of the hot milk into the eggs to temper them. Pour the eggs into the pan and cook over medium-low heat, whisking constantly, for 5 minutes, or until it has simmered for 2 minutes. Strain through a fine-mesh sieve into a bowl and stir in the vanilla. Place the bowl in the ice water bath and stir occasionally for 15 to 20 minutes, or until cold.

Place the white chocolate in a microwave-safe bowl and microwave on high heat for 1 minute, then stir. If the chocolate is not all melted, place it back in the microwave for 15 seconds at a time, stirring after each time, until it is completely melted. Let cool until lukewarm.

Place the heavy cream in a large bowl and beat with an electric mixer for 3 minutes, or until soft peaks form. (When the beaters are lifted out of the cream, they form peaks that fold over when the beaters pull away.)

Stir the white chocolate into the pudding with a spatula. Fold one quarter of the whipped cream into the pudding to loosen it, then gently but thoroughly fold in remaining whipped cream.

To assemble the cake: Carefully cut the cooled cake with a bread knife, splitting it in half to form two layers. Place one of the cake layers in the bottom of a 9-inch springform pan. Arrange half of the raspberries on the cake and gently spread half of the mousse over the raspberries, being careful not to move them around. Place the remaining cake layer over the mousse and press firmly to remove any air pockets. Spread the remaining mousse over the cake and arrange the remaining raspberries on top of the mousse. Refrigerate for at least 6 hours before serving.

I know you're thinking "Soufflé? Isn't that hard to make?" Or maybe that's just me . . . Anyways, soufflés are, surprisingly enough, quite easy to make and, again, very impressive to serve. Since everyone seems to make chocolate soufflé, we thought we would do vanilla instead and serve it with a chocolate sauce.

VANILLA SOUFFLÉ WITH CHOCOLATE SAUCE

SERVES 6

SOUFFLÉ

1/4 cup butter

5 tablespoons flour

Pinch of salt

1 cup milk

3 eggs

1/3 cup sugar

1 teaspoon vanilla

CHOCOLATE SAUCE

2/3 cup chocolate chips

1/2 cup heavy cream

1/4 cup sugar

KITCHEN SHORTCUT

Use 1/2 cup of prepared chocolate sauce and omit the chocolate sauce ingredients and preparation.

To prepare the soufflé: Preheat the oven to 325°F. Lightly butter the bottoms of six 6-ounce ramekins or custard dishes.

Place the butter in a large saucepan and cook over medium-high heat for 1 minute, or until the butter is melted. Add the flour and salt and stir until combined. Gradually add the milk and cook, stirring constantly, for 2 minutes, or until thick. Remove from the heat and let cool.

Separate the eggs, placing the whites and yolks in separate bowls. Whip the egg yolks with an electric mixer on medium-high speed for 2 minutes, or until thick and lemon colored. Add the sugar and stir into the milk mixture.

Clean the beaters and beat the egg whites with an electric mixer for 2 minutes, or until soft peaks form. (When the beaters are lifted out of the whites, they form peaks that fold over when the beaters pull away.) Gently fold the egg whites and vanilla into the saucepan until just combined. Spoon the soufflé into the prepared ramekins and place them in a baking pan. Put the baking pan in the oven and carefully add 1 inch of hot water to create a water bath. Bake for 25 to 35 minutes, or until a knife inserted in the center of the soufflés comes out clean.

Meanwhile, prepare the chocolate sauce: Place the chocolate chips, cream, and sugar in a small saucepan and cook over low heat, stirring frequently, for 5 minutes, or until the chocolate is melted and the sugar is dissolved. Remove from the heat and serve warm.

To finish the soufflés: Remove the soufflés from the water bath using tongs and place each one on a serving plate. Poke a hole in the center of each warm soufflé with a spoon and pour in a little of the chocolate sauce. Serve immediately.

KITCHEN HISTORY

The soufflé was created in Paris in 1782. It was first included in an 1813 cookbook that promised "a new method of giving good and extremely cheap fashionable suppers at routs and soirees." So there you have it, one of the most famous desserts in history was created because it was cheap.

✳ ✳
Kitchen Tip

Soufflés should always be cooked on the bottom rack of the oven because it is generally a little hotter there and they will have plenty of room to rise.

This is a really delicious and super impressive dessert. Make this for your parents when you are trying to make up for something or buttering them up, and they're almost guaranteed to forgive and forget or say yes. The ravioli are made using wonton wrappers, so you don't have to go through all the trouble of making pasta dough.

M

NECTARINE RAVIOLI

SERVES 4

SAUCE

2 nectarines

¼ cup sugar

½ cup water

RAVIOLI

1 nectarine

¼ cup ricotta cheese

2 tablespoons sugar

1 egg yolk

16 3-inch square wonton wrappers

2 tablespoons butter

To prepare the sauce: Peel and chop the nectarines and place them in a small saucepan. Add the sugar and water and cook over medium heat for 15 minutes, or until the nectarines are soft. Place the nectarine mixture in a blender and cover the lid with a towel. Holding down the blender lid, purée until smooth. Refrigerate until ready to serve.

To prepare the ravioli: Peel the nectarine, cut it in half, and remove the pit. Cut the nectarine into 32 slices and set aside.

Place the ricotta cheese, sugar, and egg yolk in a small bowl and stir until combined.

Lay one of the wonton wrappers on a flat surface. Place 1 teaspoon of the ricotta mixture in the middle of the wonton skin and top with 2 nectarine slices. Dip your finger in water and run it over two edges of the wonton. Fold the wonton into a triangle, pressing on the sides to seal the edges. Just before sealing the last bit, gently press on the center to remove any air pockets. Repeat the process with the remaining ingredients.

Lightly butter or spray a baking pan. Bring a large pot of water to a boil. Place some of the ravioli in the boiling water and cook for 2 to 3 minutes, or until they float. Remove from the water with a slotted spoon, drain briefly on paper towels, and place on the prepared baking pan. Repeat the process with the

remaining ravioli. (The ravioli may be covered with plastic wrap and refrigerated for several hours.)

Melt the butter in a large sauté pan over medium-high heat. Add the ravioli to the pan and cook for 3 to 4 minutes on each side, or until golden brown.

Place 4 ravioli on each plate and drizzle with the nectarine sauce.

Marzipan is sweetened almond paste. You are probably most familiar with it when it is shaped into cute little animals or fruits, but it makes a great filling for cakes. These tortes have a lot of steps, but they are a really impressive dessert that would be great for some kind of celebratory dinner.

M

INDIVIDUAL ALMOND TORTES WITH MARZIPAN

SERVES 6

PUDDING

¼ cup sugar

1½ tablespoons cornstarch

Pinch of salt

1 cup milk

2 egg yolks

½ teaspoon almond extract

1 teaspoon butter

CAKE

½ cup butter

1 cup sugar

1 teaspoon vanilla

2 eggs

1 teaspoon baking powder

¼ teaspoon salt

1⅓ cups cake flour

½ cup milk

MERINGUE

4 egg whites

1 teaspoon cream of tartar

½ cup sugar

7 ounces marzipan

To prepare the pudding: Fill a large bowl about halfway with ice cubes and add enough water to almost cover the ice.

Combine the sugar, cornstarch, and salt in a saucepan. Gradually add the milk. Cook over medium-high heat, stirring frequently, for 5 minutes, or until the mixture comes to a boil. Boil for 1 minute. Beat the egg yolks slightly in a small bowl. Slowly whisk some of the hot liquid into the eggs to temper them. Pour the eggs into the pan and cook, stirring constantly, for 2 minutes, or until the mixture barely begins to bubble. (Do not allow the pudding to boil or the eggs will curdle.) Remove from the heat and stir in the almond extract and butter.

Strain the pudding into a bowl through a fine-mesh sieve and place the bowl in the ice water bath. Stir occasionally for 20 to 30 minutes, or until the pudding is cool. Remove the bowl from the ice water bath, lay a piece of plastic wrap directly on the pudding, and refrigerate for 1 hour, or until completely chilled.

To prepare the cake: Preheat the oven to 350°F. Lightly butter or spray an 11 by 17-inch baking sheet.

Place the butter and sugar in a large bowl and beat with an electric mixer on medium speed for 3 to 4 minutes, or until light and fluffy. Add the vanilla and mix for 30 seconds, or until blended. Add the eggs one at a

time, mixing after each addition until completely incorporated. Add the baking powder and salt and mix well. Alternately add the flour and milk one third at a time, mixing well after each addition. Spread the batter in the prepared pan and bake for 15 to 17 minutes, or until the center springs back when gently pressed. Remove the cake from the oven and cool in the pan.

To prepare the meringue: Raise the oven temperature to 375°F.

Place the egg whites and cream of tartar in a bowl and beat with an electric mixer on high speed for 3 minutes, or until soft peaks form. (When the beaters are lifted out of the cream, they form peaks that fold over when the beaters pull away.) Add the sugar and beat for 1 minute, or until stiff peaks form. (When the beaters are lifted out of the cream, they form peaks that remain upright.)

To assemble the tortes: Cut the marzipan into 12 slices and roll each slice into a 3-inch circle.

Cut eighteen 3-inch circles from the cake using a ring cutter or cookie cutter. Place 6 of the cakes on an ungreased baking sheet, top with a circle of marzipan, and top with a little of the pudding. Repeat the process and top with a third layer of cake. Spread the meringue over the top and sides of the tortes and bake for 10 to 12 minutes, or until the meringue is golden brown on the tips. Serve immediately.

KITCHEN HISTORY

No one is quite sure where or when people started making marzipan. But we do know that it has been around for at least 500 years. In the sixteenth century, marzipan was thought to have medicinal properties and could only be dispensed by pharmacists. We can't even imagine what they thought it cured.

This may be the coolest-looking cake ever. When I first talked about trying fondant frosting, my mom said she had heard horror stories about how hard it was to work with. But as my dad says, "No brains, no fear." So I tried it. I'm not sure what all the fuss is about: I have made it many times and it's worked perfectly every time.

WRAPPED PRESENT SPICE CAKE

SERVES 9

CAKE

1 tablespoon white wine vinegar

1 cup milk

$^1/_2$ cup butter

$^3/_4$ cup sugar

$^3/_4$ cup firmly packed brown sugar

2 eggs

1 teaspoon baking soda

1 teaspoon ground cinnamon

$^1/_2$ teaspoon ground nutmeg

$^1/_2$ teaspoon ground cloves

$^1/_2$ teaspoon salt

1$^3/_4$ cups flour

FROSTING

$^1/_2$ cup butter

6 cups confectioners' sugar

$^1/_2$ cup milk

1 teaspoon vanilla

To prepare the cake: Preheat the oven to 350°F. Lightly butter or spray two 8-inch square cake pans.

Place the vinegar in a liquid measuring cup and add enough milk to make 1 cup.

Place the butter, sugar, and brown sugar in a large bowl and beat with an electric mixer on medium speed for 2 minutes, or until creamy. Add the eggs and mix for 1 minute, or until thoroughly incorporated. Add the baking soda, cinnamon, nutmeg, cloves, and salt and mix for 30 seconds, or until combined. Alternately add the milk and flour one third at a time, mixing well after each addition. Pour half of the batter into each prepared pan and bake for 30 to 40 minutes, or until the center springs back when gently pressed.

To prepare the frosting: Place the butter in a large bowl and beat with an electric mixer on medium speed for 1 minute, or until creamy. Add the confectioners' sugar, milk, and vanilla and mix on low speed for 2 minutes, or until fluffy.

FONDANT

1/4 cup cold water

1 tablespoon unflavored gelatin

1/2 cup light corn syrup

1 tablespoon glycerin

2 tablespoons vegetable shortening

2 pounds confectioners' sugar

Red food coloring

✳ ✳ Kitchen Tip

Glycerin is used in the fondant to help keep it from drying out and to keep the sugar from crystallizing. It can be purchased wherever cake decorating supplies are sold.

To prepare the fondant: Place the water in a bowl, stir in the gelatin, and let stand for 5 minutes, or until thick. Place the gelatin in the top of a double boiler over barely simmering water and heat for 2 minutes, or until it is dissolved. Add the corn syrup and glycerin and mix well. Stir in the shortening and remove from the heat just before it is completely melted. Cool until lukewarm.

Place half of the confectioners' sugar in a large bowl and make a well in the center. Pour the gelatin mixture into the well and stir with a wooden spoon, adding additional sugar as needed until the fondant is not sticky. Place the fondant on a flat surface sprinkled with some of the remaining confectioners' sugar. Sprinkle the top of the fondant with confectioners' sugar, fold in half, and push forward slightly with the heel of your hand. Rotate the fondant a quarter turn and continue the process until the remaining confectioners' sugar is incorporated. Cut off one third of the fondant and place a few drops of food coloring on top. Continue the process of folding, pressing, and turning with this piece of fondant until the food coloring is evenly distributed.

To assemble the cake: Place 1 of the cakes upside down on a serving platter and cover the top and sides with about half the frosting. Place the remaining cake upside down on top of the frosted cake and spread the remaining frosting on the top and sides, blending the upper and lower portions of the sides as you go. Smooth the sides and top of the frosting as flat as possible.

Roll the white fondant into a 16-inch square. Roll the fondant loosely around the rolling pin and unroll it over the cake. Smooth the fondant over the top and down the sides of the cake, gently working out any

[continued]

folds or bubbles. Trim any excess fondant by running a knife around the plate at the bottom edge of the cake.

Roll the red fondant into a long rectangle about $^3/_8$ inch thick. Cut 2 strips about 2 by 16 inches, 4 strips about $^1/_4$ by 16 inches, and 1 strip about 3 by 20 inches.

Place one of the 2-inch strips down the center of the cake and arrange one of the $^1/_4$-inch-thick strips about $^1/_8$ inch away from each side of the 2 inch strip. Repeat the process going the other way to form a cross on top of the cake. Cut 5 inches off one end of the 20-inch strip. Fold the longer piece in half with the seam in the center and wrap the short piece around the center to form the bow. Place the bow at the center of the cross.

KITCHEN CHEMISTRY

Baking soda is pure sodium bicarbonate. When baking soda is combined with moisture and an acidic ingredient, such as yogurt, chocolate, or buttermilk, it immediately begins producing the carbon dioxide bubbles that make baked goods rise. So recipes that contain baking soda need to be baked right away, or they will fall flat.

As soon as we tried these in a restaurant, we knew we had to try to make them at home. It took a few tries, but we finally got it right. The only thing that could make this cake any better is a little vanilla ice cream on the side.

MOLTEN-CENTER CHOCOLATE CAKES

SERVES 8

FILLING

1/3 cup chocolate chips

1 tablespoon butter

3 tablespoons heavy cream

CAKE

1 cup chocolate chips

5 tablespoons butter

4 eggs

1/2 cup sugar

3 tablespoons flour

Pinch of salt

To prepare the filling: Place the chocolate chips in a microwave-safe bowl and microwave on high heat for 30 seconds, then stir. If the chocolate is not all melted, place it back in the microwave for 15 seconds at a time, stirring after each time, until it is completely melted. Be careful not to let the chocolate start to bubble or it will burn and get gritty. Stir in the butter and let cool to room temperature. Stir in the cream and refrigerate for 30 minutes. Beat the mixture with an electric mixer for 5 minutes, or until fluffy. Refrigerate until ready to use.

To prepare the cake: Generously butter 8 ramekins or custard dishes and place them in a baking pan.

Place the chocolate chips in a microwave-safe bowl and microwave on high heat for 1 minute, then stir. If the chocolate is not all melted, place it back in the microwave for 15 seconds at a time, stirring after each time, until it is completely melted, being careful not to let the chocolate burn. Stir in the butter and let cool slightly.

Separate the eggs, placing the yolks in a large bowl and the whites in a medium bowl. Add 1/4 cup of the sugar to the egg yolks and beat with an electric mixer for 4 to 5 minutes, or until thick and lightly colored. Stir in the melted chocolate and then the flour. Wash the beaters. Beat the egg whites on high speed for 1 minute, or until frothy. Add the remaining 1/4 cup sugar

The filling for this cake is called **ganache** (gahn-AHSH). When it is whipped as it is here, it is called **ganache soufflé** and can be used as a filling for cakes or rolled into balls for truffles. Before it's whipped, it can be poured over cakes and tortes for a smooth frosting.

and beat for 2 minutes, or until stiff peaks form. (When the beaters are lifted out of the egg whites, they form peaks that remain upright.) Stir about one fourth of the egg whites into the chocolate to loosen it, then gently fold the remaining egg whites into the chocolate mixture.

Fill each of the ramekins halfway with the batter. Place a small scoop of the filling in the center and fill about three quarters of the way with the remaining batter. Refrigerate for at least 2 hours, or until just prior to baking and serving. (The cakes may be refrigerated for up to 1 day.)

Preheat the oven to 400°F. Bake the cakes for 18 minutes, remove from the oven, and cool for 10 minutes. (The cakes will fall as they cool.) Serve immediately.

✳ Kitchen Tip ✳

Egg whites need to be gently folded into other ingredients to keep them from deflating. Use a spatula and run it down one side of the bowl, across the bottom, and up the other side, and fold the ingredients over the egg whites. Turn the bowl slightly and continue the process until the egg whites are fairly well blended. It is better to have a few streaks of egg white than to overmix.

I know we keep saying this, but this dessert looks great and is really easy to make. Honest. Just make sure to line the pan with parchment paper. It may seem like no big deal, but if you skip it, I guarantee the center of the cake will stick to the pan.

CHOCOLATE-CARAMEL-PECAN TORTE

SERVES 8

TORTE

1 cup chocolate chips

2 tablespoons butter

1 cup flour

1 cup sugar

1 teaspoon baking powder

½ teaspoon salt

¾ cup milk

1 egg

½ teaspoon vanilla

TOPPINGS

¾ cup pecan halves

½ cup sugar

¼ cup water

½ cup heavy cream

2 tablespoons butter

To prepare the torte: Preheat the oven to 350°F. Cut a parchment paper circle to fit in the bottom of a 9-inch cake pan. Lightly butter or spray the parchment paper and the sides of the pan.

Place the chocolate chips in a microwave-safe bowl and microwave on high heat for 1 minute, then stir. If the chocolate is not all melted, place it back in the microwave for 15 seconds at a time, stirring after each time, until it is completely melted. Be careful not to let the chocolate start to bubble or it will burn and get gritty. Stir in the butter and let cool slightly.

Stir together the flour, sugar, baking powder, and salt in a large bowl. Add half of the milk and mix with an electric mixer on low speed for 2 minutes, until airy. Add the remaining milk, the egg, the melted chocolate, and the vanilla and mix for 2 minutes. Pour the batter into the prepared pan and bake for 45 to 50 minutes, or until a toothpick inserted in the center comes out clean. (The torte will form a crust on top that you will have to poke through to test.) Leave the oven on at 350°F.

Remove the torte from the pan and cool on a wire rack.

To prepare the toppings: Place the pecans on a baking sheet and toast in the oven for 10 minutes, or until they are lightly browned.

**KITCHEN
SHORTCUT**
Warm 1 cup of prepared
caramel sauce in the
microwave and omit the
caramel sauce ingredi-
ents and preparation.

Place the sugar in a small saucepan and pour in the
water, making sure all of the sugar gets wet. Cook over
medium-high heat, without stirring, for 10 minutes, or
until the sugar turns golden brown. Add the cream and
butter to the pan and stir until smooth. (The sugar may
harden when you add the cream, but continue cooking
and it will melt again.)

Place the torte on a serving platter and spoon half of
the caramel over the top. Arrange the pecan halves
around the top of the torte and drizzle the remaining
caramel over the pecans.

This is a really light dessert, perfect for when raspberries are in season. Tuiles are just really thin cookies. For this dessert we left them flat, but they can be rolled or shaped while they are still warm. Although the individual pieces can be prepared in advance, the whole dessert has to be put together at the last minute or the tuiles will get soggy.

FRESH RASPBERRY NAPOLEONS

SERVES 6

TUILES

¹/₃ cup flour

¹/₄ cup sugar

5 tablespoons butter, melted

3 egg whites

¹/₂ teaspoon vanilla

SAUCE

1 cup heavy cream

2 egg yolks

2 tablespoons sugar

1 teaspoon vanilla

2 pints (4 cups) fresh
   raspberries

To prepare the tuiles: Preheat the oven to 300°F. Lightly oil or spray a baking sheet.

Place the flour and sugar in a bowl. Add the melted butter, egg whites, and vanilla and stir until smooth. Spread the batter into very thin 3¹/₂-inch circles on the prepared baking sheet. Bake for 8 to 10 minutes, or until golden brown. Immediately remove the tuiles from the pan and cool on parchment or waxed paper. Repeat the process with the remaining batter to form 18 tuiles. (The tuiles can be stored in an airtight container for several days.)

To prepare the sauce: Place the cream in a small saucepan and cook over medium-high heat for 3 minutes, or until it comes to a boil. Whisk together the egg yolks and sugar and slowly whisk some of the hot cream into the eggs to temper them. Pour the eggs into the cream and cook over medium-low heat, stirring constantly, for 1 minute, or until it coats the back of a metal spoon. (Do not allow the sauce to boil or the eggs will curdle.) Remove from the heat, stir in the vanilla, and strain the sauce through a fine-mesh sieve. (The sauce may be served warm or cooled in an ice water bath and refrigerated until ready to use.)

To assemble the napoleons: Place 1 of the tuiles in the center of each plate. Arrange some of the raspberries on the tuile and top with a little of the sauce. Repeat the process to form 2 complete layers. Top the final layer with a tuile and place a raspberry in the center. Spoon the remaining sauce over the tuile, allowing it to drip down the sides of the napoleon.

Kitchen Vocab

Tuile (TWEEL) is the French word for "tile." Tuiles are thin, crisp cookies that can be left flat, rolled, or made into other shapes while they are still warm.

✳ Kitchen Tip ✳

A dish like this looks much nicer if the tuiles are all the same size. We use the top from a sour cream container and cut a circle in the center. Then we spread the batter inside the circle the same thickness as the plastic. That way all of the tuiles come out round and even in thickness.

M

TURTLE EMPANADAS

SERVES 6

CARAMEL SAUCE

½ cup sugar

¼ cup water

½ cup heavy cream

2 tablespoons butter

To prepare the caramel sauce: Place the sugar in a small saucepan and pour in the water, making sure all of the sugar gets wet. Cook over medium-high heat, without stirring, for 10 minutes, or until the sugar is golden brown. Add the cream and butter to the pan and stir until smooth. (The sugar may harden when you add the cream, but continue cooking and it will melt again.)

CHOCOLATE SAUCE

1/3 cup chocolate chips

1/4 cup heavy cream

2 tablespoons sugar

EMPANADAS

1/2 cup chopped pecans

2 sheets puff pastry

1/2 cup chocolate chips

1 egg

KITCHEN SHORTCUT

Use 1 cup of prepared caramel sauce and omit the caramel sauce ingredients and preparation.

Use 1/2 cup of prepared chocolate sauce and omit the chocolate sauce ingredients and preparation.

To prepare the chocolate sauce: Place the chocolate chips, cream, and sugar in a small saucepan and cook over low heat, stirring frequently, for 5 minutes, or until the chocolate is melted and the sugar is dissolved. Remove from the heat and cool for 10 to 15 minutes to allow it to thicken.

To prepare the empanadas: Preheat the oven to 400°F.

Place the pecans on a baking sheet and toast in the oven for 10 minutes, or until lightly browned.

Cut each sheet of puff pastry into 9 squares. Place a few of the pecans and chocolate chips in the center of each square. Lightly beat the egg and brush some on the edges of each square. Fold the squares into triangles and press down to seal the edges. Place the triangles on an ungreased baking sheet and brush the tops with the remaining egg. Bake for 12 to 15 minutes, or until golden brown.

Place 3 of the triangles on each plate and drizzle the caramel and chocolate sauces over the empanadas.

KITCHEN HISTORY

Puff pastry was an invention of Renaissance cooks. This description of rolling out the dough came from a seventeenth-century cookbook: "drive out the piece with a rolling pin, and do with butter one piece by another, and then fold your paste upon the butter and drive it out again, and do so five or six times together." That one sounds cool, but our favorite line is, "the paste had to be driven out so thin that ye may blow it up from the table." No wonder we buy it frozen.

Index